Euthanasia

Euthanasia
Spiritual, Medical & Legal
Issues in Terminal Health Care

BETH SPRING
& ED LARSON

MULTNOMAH

Portland, Oregon 97266

Edited by Rodney L. Morris
Cover design and illustration by Britt Taylor Collins

EUTHANASIA
© 1988 by Beth Spring and Ed Larson
Published by Multnomah Press
Portland, Oregon 97266

Multnomah Press is a ministry of Multnomah School of the Bible, 8435 Northeast Glisan Street, Portland, Oregon 97220.

Printed in the United States of America

Library of Congress Cataloging-in-Publication Data

Spring, Beth
Euthanasia/ by Beth Spring and Ed Larson.
   p.   cm.
  Includes bibliographies and index.
  ISBN 0-88070-254-0 (pbk.).
   1. Euthanasia—Moral and ethical aspects. 2. Terminal care—Moral and ethical aspects. 3. Euthanasia—Religious aspects-
-Christianity. I. Larson, Ed. II.Title.
R726.S67 1988
174'.24—dc19   88-5357
                                                   CIP

88 89 90 91 92 93 94 95 - 10 9 8 7 6 5 4 3 2

Dedicated to

A Grandmother,
Gertrude Lux,
and
A Godson,
Daniel Weikart
Whose lives have been physically blessed
by modern medical technology

Contents

Acknowledgments

This book reflects the assistance and support of many people and organizations. We wish to express our gratitude and acknowledge our debt to at least a few of them.

Several outstanding experts in the ethical, legal, and medical issues raised by terminal health-care decisions have generously given us the benefit of their time and insight. They include Dr. Rob Roy MacGregor, U.S. Surgeon General C. Everett Koop, Edward R. Grant, Dr. J. A. J. Stevens, Judith Wilson Ross, David Moberg, Dr. Abigail Rian Evans, and Father Richard Gula, S. S. Other individuals who contributed ideas and sources of information include Joyce Terry, Johanna Turner, Judy Shelly, Roberta Paige, and McKendree Langley. Although their contributions immeasurably strengthened this book, they are not responsible for any of its weaknesses.

Organizations have contributed to our work in various ways. Supportive resources and services were provided by Families for Responsible Educational Environment and Christian Conciliation Service of Puget Sound. Research and reference materials were provided by the National Institutes of Health, The Hastings Center, the Society for the Right to Die, the Massachusetts Supreme Court, the Library of Congress, Catholic University, Georgetown University's Kennedy Institute of Ethics, Hospice of Northern Virginia, the National Hospice Organization, and the National Right to Life Committee.

Early opportunities to develop our ideas were provided by *Christianity Today* and the Evangelical Round Table, hosted by Eastern College. Multnomah Press provided vital ongoing assistance and support, especially through the expert editorial skill of Rodney Morris and the typing services of Sydne Ebel.

Finally, we wish to thank our family and friends for their patient support and encouragement throughout this project. Without them, this book would have been impossible.

Introduction

Coma. Paralysis. Inoperable cancer. Alzheimer's disease. Permanent brain damage. Severely handicapped newborn. Terminal condition.

Some of us face these dreaded circumstances ourselves or in the lives of our loved ones. How, in the press of crisis and grief, do we respond? Even if we never face these agonizing issues personally, do we still have a responsibility to take a stand? Does it matter if society permits or encourages certain ways of handling these dilemmas? The questions have no easy answers.

Lutheran Bishop Lowell O. Erdahl tells the story of a mother who gave birth to premature twins whose survival depended on life-support systems. "One child, though tiny, was normal; the other was blind and severely deformed. As the mother looked at the normal child, she thanked God for the medical technology that enabled hope for a full and meaningful life, but as she looked at the deformed child who seemed destined for a world of darkness and suffering, she silently cursed the same technology that sustained its life."[1]

11

Most people do not experience these contrasting reactions quite so strikingly, yet the use of life-sustaining technology provokes deeply felt and sharply different responses. Situations like this one, and the much more prevalent cases of the terminally ill or chronically ill elderly, are often met with the suggestion that "mercy killing" would offer the suffering patient a "good death."

Euthanasia, putting a person to death by a deliberate act or omission, is the subject of this book. It provokes real controversy in courts and legislatures, confronts families and physicians, and challenges theologians and ethicists. The debate is colored by advancing medical technologies, changes in doctor-patient relationships, and population trends. The AIDS epidemic, requests for assisted suicide, and the influence of popular media vie for attention. Living wills, hospice care, and court-appointed surrogates now enter the picture.

SOME CASE HISTORIES

The following actual cases illustrate a few of the various ways decisions involving the use of life-sustaining procedures can confront a person, a family, or a religious institution. They also show how responses can vary.

A Patient: Sidney Hook

In 1984, Sidney Hook was ready to die. Weakened by a serious stroke, paralyzed on one side, tormented for days with violent hiccups that prevented eating, and suffering from an awful pleurisy that made him feel as if he were drowning, Hook gave up. In his eighties at the time, he had already lived a remarkably full life as one of America's leading philosophers and educators.

Hook had written and lectured about human freedom and dignity for over half a century. "It is better to be a live jackal than a dead lion—for jackals, not men," he once wrote. "Those who are prepared to live like men and, if necessary, die like men, have the best prospect of surviving as free men and escaping the fate of both jackals and lions."[2]

Racked with illness and confined to a hospital bed, Hook decided that the struggle to survive was no longer worth the effort. He asked his physician to end all life-sustaining medical procedures for him. The physician refused, saying it was premature. "A month later, I was discharged from the hospital," Hook recounted. "In six months, I regained the use of my limbs. I have resumed my writing and research." In 1985, he received the Medal of Freedom from President Reagan. Two years later, he published yet another book and several articles. Clearly, Hook had no longer given up.

Despite his recovery, Hook maintained afterward that the doctor should have honored his request. Elderly people, who have little to gain, should be allowed to avoid the agony he suffered, Hook argued in a widely distributed newspaper article. He was surprised by the volume of mail he received in response to this article, with almost all of the letters supporting his stance and many of them describing similar situations involving relatives. A few letters dissented, however, and talked about the sanctity of all life. Hook responded that when life becomes so undignified, there is nothing sacred about it.[3]

A Wife: Edith Schaeffer

On Easter Sunday of 1984, the time had come for Edith Schaeffer to decide. Her husband, the world-famous Christian apologist Francis Schaeffer, had been ill with cancer for several years. As his condition worsened, the Schaeffers moved from their long-time residence in Switzerland to a new home near the Mayo Clinic in Rochester, Minnesota. Extensive treatment allowed Francis to write and lecture until very near the end. But now final treatment decisions had to be made, and Francis was no longer able to make them himself.

Six physicians called Mrs. Schaeffer aside at the Clinic, and the leading consultant said, "He is dying of the advancing cancer. Do you want him to be placed in intensive care on machines? Now is the time to make the choice."

"You men have already done great things during these last years and these last few weeks. You fought for life and gave Fran time to complete an amazing amount of work," Edith Schaeffer replied, reflecting on the distinction her husband had drawn between preserving life at all costs and simply prolonging death. Now, however, Edith realized the time had come for Francis to go home, surrounded by the familiar things he loved.

Soon Francis was home, in a bedroom with large windows overlooking colorful flowers, budding trees, and feeding birds. Treasured memorabilia from Switzerland filled the room, and the favorite music of Beethoven, Bach, Schubert, and Handel flooded the air. Ten days after leaving the hospital, with the sounds of Handel's *Messiah* still in the air, Francis Schaeffer died.[4]

A Daughter: Betty Rollin

New York news correspondent and writer Betty Rollin watched as her seventy-eight-year-old mother was slowly, painfully dying of ovarian cancer. In 1981, an excruciating series of eight chemotherapy treatments arrested the disease at an agonizing cost in pain and suffering.

When the cancer returned two years later, it appeared to be terminal. Again chemotherapy was the only option. An initial series of three treatments was prescribed, with three more likely to follow.

"Mother, you don't have to. No one can force you to have chemotherapy. You can decide not to," Rollin cried.

"How can I decide not to?" her mother replied. "It's the only chance I have."

This faint hope gradually withered. After only two treatments, she was too weak to receive more. From then on, she grew gradually worse and needed constant care either at her apartment or in a hospital. Although hired attendants provided the basic care, Rollin visited regularly.

"I've had a wonderful life, but now it's over, or it should be. I'm not afraid to die but I'm afraid of this illness, what it's doing to me. I'm not better; I'm worse. There's never any relief from it now. Nothing but nausea and this pain. The pain—it never stops," her mother confessed one day to Rollin. "This isn't life. If I had life I'd want it. I don't want this."

Following these comments, and after personal reflection, Rollin began researching a way to help her mother die. After extensive research, Rollin found a doctor in the Netherlands (where active euthanasia is regularly practiced) who recommended appropriate drugs to kill her mother painlessly. The key drug, nembutal, could be obtained through her mother's regular physician as a pain-killer. Rollin passed the word to her mother, who convinced the physician to prescribe the potentially lethal medication.

From then on, her mother took charge with Rollin acting as agent. Final affairs were put in order and arrangements made over several days. Her mother was then at home, tended by nurses. On the appointed day, the night nurse reported that the patient slept well and woke cheerful. The day nurse also found the patient cheerful. She was still strong enough to eat, dress, walk, and think clearly.

Rollin arrived in the afternoon, and the nurse was sent home early. Rollin's husband came a little later. The three looked at photographs together and discussed old times. Then, while Rollin watched, her mother took the drugs as directed by the Dutch doctor. "You're doing it, Mother," Rollin whispered. "You're doing it. You're doing great." After swallowing all the pills, her mother looked at Rollin and remarked, "Remember, I am the most happy woman. And this is my wish."[5]

A Christian Institution: Crista Nursing Center

Seattle's premiere Christian home for the elderly, Crista Senior Community, is run by Crista Ministries as part of a far-reaching, $30-million nondenominational organization that includes a leading relief agency (World Concern) and a service providing listings of Christian vocational opportunities (Intercristo).

In 1985, a seventy-four-year-old woman in Crista's nursing center suffered strokes that left her unable to swallow food and water. Tubes were needed to provide her nutrition and hydration. Her family obtained medical certification that she had no chance of recovering and a physician's directive for the nursing center to remove her feeding tube.

Three nurses refused on ethical and religious grounds to obey the directive. They were asked to resign, but this request was rescinded, and Crista refused the family's instructions. A court order was obtained by the family, and the patient was moved to another facility where the feeding tube was removed and she died.

Two months later, another patient's family also ordered an end to artificial feeding. This time the patient was moved to another unit within the Crista facility where the nurses did not object to the order. The patient died about a week after her feeding tube was removed.

Extensive media coverage followed, and contributions to Crista's many ministries temporarily dropped. One nurse later resigned over the incident and filed an employment lawsuit against the organization.[6]

Crista's Board of Trustees appointed a blue-ribbon committee to review policy in this area. Based on that committee's report, the Board adopted in mid-1987 formal guidelines regarding life-sustaining treatment. In these guidelines, food, water, and oxygen were characterized as "natural supports" for life and were to be provided as needed unless detrimental to other aspects of the patient's physical well-being. Other life-sustaining procedures could be ended if, but only if, death was imminent from an irreversible illness. The primary care nurse was to be consulted on these matters in addition to family members and physicians. (The complete guidelines appear in Appendix 1 of this book.)

Perhaps most critically, policies adopted by Crista encourage patients to consider their wishes regarding life-sustaining treatment before a terminal illness strikes, and to decide these matters for themselves while they still can. Crista recommends that patients consult with their pastors in making such decisions.

A Mother: Dotty McClure

Dotty McClure's son Michael developed hydrocephalus, or water on the brain, at age twenty-one. After shunts were installed in his skull to relieve the pressure, Michael found work and moved into his own apartment near the family home in Sheboygan, Wisconsin.

One day in 1985, Mrs. McClure felt an uncommon urge to call her son. "I never did that before. I never called—he's of age," she noted later. "But somebody up there told me to call." No one answered. She rushed to his apartment and found him sitting on the floor of his closet deep in a coma. One of the shunts had clogged, and rising fluid pressures had affected his brain.

Michael was rushed to a hospital and remained there for four months, but his condition never changed. Physicians at the hospital told Mrs. McClure her son would probably not regain consciousness and asked to place him in a nursing home. She objected and obtained legal custody over her adult son so that she could take him home to live.

She nursed Michael at home every day for nine more months. She fed him through a tube inserted directly into his stomach, and even replaced the tube six times. She dressed him in regular clothes every day and in pajamas every night. She played music for him on his stereo and turned on the television for him. She toileted him, bathed him, turned him, and kept his artificial breathing devices functioning. She talked to him constantly. "Being Irish, I talk a lot," Mrs. McClure confided. But he never answered; he never responded.

Before dawn one summer morning in 1986, as his mother slept on the floor next to his bed, Michael woke up and exclaimed, "Ma, where are you?" He was wide awake and hungry. Dotty McClure sat up dumbfounded, and then cried for joy. She had her son back. Within months, he was totally recovered.

"I knew deep down he would wake up. But if it took twenty or forty years, I was willing to wait," Dotty McClure said later. "I was going to fight to death to bring him around."[7]

———— • ————

These stories are not ordinary. Decisions involving the use or nonuse of life-sustaining procedures are never ordinary. They are becoming more common, however, with the advance of medical technology and the re-evaluation of medical, legal, and ethical standards.

Most people would prefer not to think about terminal health-care decisions, especially for themselves. Yet everyone lives with the risk of the issue arising without warning for themselves or relatives, when it may be too late to think clearly or make binding decisions. This book addresses the current medical, social, and legal situation, reviews religious and ethical considerations, and suggests possible responses. Easy answers do not exist, but the questions cannot be avoided.

Introduction, Notes
_____

1. Lowell O. Erdahl, *Pro-Life/Pro-Peace: Life-Affirming Alternatives to Abortion, War, Mercy Killing, and the Death Penalty* (Minneapolis: Augsburg Publishing House, 1986), 105.

2. Sidney Hook, *Political Power and Personal Freedom: Critical Studies in Democracy, Communism, and Civil Rights* (New York: Collier Books, 1962), 5.

3. Sidney Hook, "In Defense of Voluntary Euthanasia," *New York Times,* 1 March 1987, sec. 4; and Sidney Hook, Interview, 14 August 1987.

4. Edith Schaeffer, *Forever Music* (Nashville: Thomas Nelson Publishers, 1986), 62-63.

5. Betty Rollin, *Last Wish* (New York: Linden Press, 1985), 91-92, 149-50, and 134-35; and Ron Given and Linda Prout, "Mercy—or Murder," *Newsweek,* 9 September 1985, 25.

6. Ed Larson and Beth Spring, "Life-Defying Acts: Do Modern Medical Technologies Sustain Life or Merely Prolong Dying?" *Christianity Today,* 6 March 1987, 17-18, 22; and Ron Powell, "Two Families' Decisions: Letting Loved Ones Starve," *Seattle Times/Seattle Post Intelligencer,* 14 April 1985, sec. A.

7. Dotty McClure, in "Donahue" transcript no. 11206, Multimedia Entertainment, Inc., 3-6, 10.

PART 1

THE SITUATION

The news media regularly highlight dramatic stories involving life-threatening illnesses and injuries. Some of these stories describe the implantation of artificial hearts, publicize nationwide searches for infant organ donors, or recount other heroic medical efforts to save lives. Other stories relate seemingly miraculous healings, such as the waking of a long-term coma victim. An increasing number of stories report the termination of life-sustaining medical procedures for a seriously ill patient, or even the mercy-killing or suicide of a dying person.

The first part of this book examines the medical, societal, and legal developments behind these news stories. Chapter 1 explores some of the new medical realities of aging and health care that confront us now—the good news as well as the challenges. In chapter 2, we discuss how these medical realities are influencing social attitudes. Is America well on the way toward accepting euthanasia? The final chapter of this part reviews laws and court rulings that govern the use of modern medical procedures and enforce societal standards in health care and human rights.

Part 2 outlines ethical and religious considerations under-lying and informing the euthanasia debate. Possible individual responses to these developments are suggested in Part 3, includ-ing creative alternatives for people approaching the end of life. As we will see, the rapidly increasing capacity of medical technology to preserve life and prolong death has raised ethical, spiritual, and legal questions that our society is only now begin-ning to tackle—and is far from solving.

Chapter 1

Changes and Choices:
The Medical Realities of Aging and Health Care

*F*ew of us need to be reminded that we are growing older. Whether it's a birthday card with a not-so-subtle message about aging or a furtive search in the mirror for gray hairs, the signs of aging crop up all around us. Just as individuals navigate a life course that leads inevitably to old age, the U.S. population too is growing older. Landmark shifts in the proportion of elderly Americans to young and middle-aged citizens are rapidly approaching. The demographic changes in our midst are in part the result of amazing advances in medical technique and technology. More than any generation before us, we tend to be healthy, alert, and productive for decades beyond the age of sixty-five.

That is the good news. There is a challenge implicit in these changes as well—a challenge to physicians, families, churches, hospitals, lawyers, and many others. An aging population is apt to encounter more chronic disease and to require long-term care, perhaps in an institution. Health care costs are escalating, and at the same time families are shrinking in size. There are fewer children per family and a higher rate of divorce than America has seen in the past. A pressing question confronts us: How will America meet the future challenge of elderly citizens in need of extended treatment and care? What will we think of the "new majority" of elderly citizens in our midst? Will we revise our stereotypes of the aged or view these individuals as a burden?

Some of America's best known elderly citizens already are setting the tone for a revised outlook on aging. Ronald Reagan, America's oldest president, turned seventy-five during his second term in office and marked the date as "the 36th anniversary of my 39th birthday." He joked with reporters at an annual dinner, "Since I came to the White House, I've gotten two hearing aids, a colon operation, skin cancer, a prostate operation and I was shot. . . . I've never felt better in my life."[1]

Squaring the Pyramid

America has been a "young" nation all its life. That will begin to change as our most numerous generation of citizens approaches the traditional retirement age. The baby boomers—people born between the years of 1945 and 1965—will begin reaching age sixty-five in 2010. That landmark, combined with lower birth rates, will set us on a course where the number of people over sixty-five is equal to or greater than any other age category.

Demographers refer to this as "squaring the pyramid." Traditionally, the U.S. population grouped by age has formed a pyramid, with greater numbers of young people than adults or senior citizens. The pyramid tapered toward the top, with relatively few people reaching their seventies or eighties. In recent years this has begun to change. In 1950, for instance, 12.4 million Americans were over sixty-five. By 1980, however, that figure had more than doubled to 25.7 million.[2]

As the birth rate began to fall, the pyramid began resembling a diamond shape. The image that perhaps best captures the effect of the baby boom on the U.S. population is the "pig in the python," slowly bulging its way through the system.

By 2030, the pyramid is expected to be completely rectangular, with roughly equivalent numbers of people in each five-year age category from birth to age seventy. The population over sixty-five will grow rapidly, to a projected 35 million in 2000 and 64 million in 2030.[3] In 1980 the proportion of the population over sixty-five stood at 11.3 percent. By 2030 this age group will represent more than 21 percent of the total population.[4]

Not only will our population as a whole consist of more elderly people, but this age group itself will experience increased longevity. Already a man who turns sixty-five can expect fourteen more years of life; a woman at sixty-five can expect to live another nineteen years.[5] As more and more people survive past the ages of seventy-five and eighty-five, new perspectives on their diverse needs and abilities are coming into focus. The "young-old," from sixty-five to seventy-four, are less likely to be considered "over the hill." In fact, people in this age category are often at the height of their ability and influence. Billy Graham, born in 1918, is still vigorously responding to God's call on his life.

The "middle-old," ages seventy-five to eighty-four, are typified by Ronald Reagan and by evangelical theologian Carl F. H. Henry. Slowed only slightly by advancing age, Henry continues to lecture worldwide, teach at colleges and universities, and write prolifically.

The so-called "old-old," those past eighty-five, tend to rely more on their grown children or other caregivers for certain tasks of daily living. As faculties such as hearing, vision, and mobility decline, this group needs care and compassion in increasing measure. By 2050, one in every twenty persons may be past eighty-five. The current figure is approximately one in one hundred[6]. Increasing numbers of the "old-old" will have living sons and daughters who themselves are past sixty-five.

Preserving Life and Health

Advances in medical knowledge and innovation in recent years forestall many of the debilitating diseases and conditions that have haunted old age in previous generations. Often, life-threatening medical emergencies of a few years ago pose a routine challenge at major medical centers.

Consider this hypothetical case study: Mrs. Melton, age sixty-seven, is hosting a Thanksgiving family reunion. In the midst of hurrying to prepare a holiday dinner, she collapses with an apparent heart attack. Her son-in-law dials 911, and in five minutes an ambulance arrives with trained paramedics on board. Mrs. Melton is rushed to a metropolitan hospital, where an emergency room diagnosis indicates she has a blood clot partially blocking the flow of blood to a section of the heart muscle. Already, Mrs. Melton may be considered fortunate. Approximately 20 percent of heart-attack victims who reach the hospital alive die because of severe damage to the heart muscle.[7] If they live, the prospects for a more complete recovery are better now than ever before.

In his book *America's Health in the Balance*, Dr. Howard H. Hiatt asserts, "Until recently doctors could treat with varying success the effects of the heart attack—the pain, the disturbances in the beating of the heart, the shock sometimes caused, and other complications. But they were helpless to deal with the clots that caused the obstruction; they stood by as events played out to see who would die, who would be left disabled, and who would recover fully."[8]

Not so today. Mrs. Melton arrives in the emergency room, and within fifteen minutes a cardiac specialist is ready to begin treatment. He places a thin tube in an artery in Mrs. Melton's leg, working it toward her heart. A dye is injected into the tube, making it possible for the doctor to view her coronary arteries with the help of X-rays projected on a television screen. This procedure, known as an angiogram, shows the doctors exactly where the clot in Mrs. Melton's heart is located.

Next the specialist uses a chemical that can dissolve newly formed clots, introducing it into the narrow tube. As he and his team peer at the television screen, they see the flow of blood slowly return to normal in Mrs. Melton's obstructed heart chamber. After observing her carefully for several more minutes, the specialist heads for the hallway, removing his mask and gloves, to deliver good news to an anxious, waiting family.

If the chemical had failed to work, heart specialists have developed another procedure for removing clots, known as angioplasty. This is done by inflating a small balloon at the end of the tube traveling through the patient's artery. In this way, the clot is dislodged and the inner walls of the blocked artery are stretched to permit a normal flow of blood.

After a few days of observation in the hospital's intensive care unit, Mrs. Melton is released in a wheelchair and returns home. A program of gentle exercise and regular neighborhood walks begins within two weeks, and she regains most of her former vigor and strength rapidly. Mrs. Melton has been the recipient of a whole chain of improvements and innovation in emergency health care that have developed in her lifetime: quick and capable transport to a modern hospital, immediate attention in the emergency room from a heart specialist, a successful treatment to correct the cause of her heart failure and not just its symptoms, and helpful follow-up treatment and therapy.

Other heart difficulties are combated now with a sophisticated array of techniques, including pacemakers, new drug therapy, transplants, and microsurgery. An emphasis on preventive measures that include no smoking, regular exercise, and a change in diet have reduced the incidence of heart attack substantially. But cardiovascular disease is still the leading killer of Americans each year.[9]

Improvements in the treatment of heart disease are matched by other remarkable advances in medicine. Along with better hygiene, a cleaner environment, and more attention to maintaining health from an early age, recent technical innovations include artificial hip joints, techniques for removing cataracts and implanting artificial lenses in the eye, and organ transplants. It is no wonder that families like the Meltons marvel at the superior, successful treatment their elderly loved one received. They experienced the best that modern medicine in America has to offer.

A Health Care Dilemma

Two hard realities have accompanied America's technical advances against disease, and both of them pose a challenge for health-care providers and society at large. One is the increasingly impersonal way doctors and patients (and their families) relate to one another, particularly in crisis situations where specialists are called in. The traditional "realm of trust" between a patient and his lifelong "family doctor" has eroded. Second, an unforeseen explosion in health care costs places a heavy burden on the elderly, the chronically ill, and their loved ones. Attitudes that arise out of these two realities, as well as heightened expectations based on medical miracles such as treatment for heart attack, may make us vulnerable to the arguments supporting the "right to die." These attitudes will be explored in full in chapter 2. For now, let's consider these two aspects of health care.

Impersonal health care. Leaps in medical knowledge and technology have given rise to a cadre of specialists. Returning to the case of Mrs. Melton, notice that the cardiologist who attended her had most likely never met her before. Her regular doctor, perhaps a general practitioner or internist, would as a matter of course refer her—or any other patient with a specific problem—to a competent specialist today.

This is a relatively recent development, and it is causing the role of the physician, and the patient's attitude toward him, to change radically. Dr. Rob Roy MacGregor, chief of the infectious diseases section at the University of Pennsylvania School of Medicine, offers some historical perspective:

> Until around 1900, there was very little a doctor could do to affect the course of any disease. For example, with the development of anesthesia, he could cut off limbs that were gangrenous or remove gallstones.
>
> But the physician in that day was primarily a counselor and the interpreter of disease, conducting the patient through the course of the illness. Today he

is a soldier—an aggressor against disease. We've
become technocrats, and to a large extent have lost
the sense of being ministers to people who are suffering.[10]

The result for the patient, MacGregor says, can be "a de-
humanizing spiral in which each organ failure is met by still
another life-support procedure."[11]

Overwhelmed by the technical assault on their loved one's
disease, the family finds it increasingly difficult to understand
what is being done and why. The patient and his closest relatives
are generally thought to be in control, to the greatest degree
possible, of decisions regarding treatment and care. But the
difficulty of comprehending and assessing various treatment
options and uncertain scenarios for recovery leave the family
at a distinct disadvantage. Frequently they do not have the
technical expertise or the knowledge to grasp all the factors
influencing treatment decisions. Meanwhile time pressures
force rapid consideration.

Suppose, for example, that our fictitious Mrs. Melton
was eighty-seven years old instead of sixty-seven. Suppose
she had been hospitalized for one year, needing regular dialysis
for her failing kidneys and being treated for a series of infections
that had left her weak and wasted. At this point, she suffers a
heart attack. The medical specialists who are called in to attend
to her would likely apply the same "full court press" to save
her as they would a younger patient in excellent health.

In cases such as this, the primary care physician and the
family may believe that the best decision is to "let nature take
its course." People do die of heart attacks after all, and if
eighty-seven-year-old Mrs. Melton had not been hospitalized
to begin with, the chances are great that she would have died
shortly after cardiac arrest. In the years before advanced medical treatment and swift medical transport made "miraculous"
treatment possible, questions regarding the choices involved
in her care would never have come up. Now they do, and they
will continue to increase in frequency and complexity.

Is it euthanasia to decide in advance, or even at the time of a medical emergency, to fail to resuscitate a patient? Are doctors "playing God" if they withhold or even withdraw a particular treatment? The views of key people debating these issues will be explored in chapter 4. But the important point here is this: These questions are real ones, and they confront real people daily. The advances in medical prowess have, in many cases, pushed us to the edge of an ethical precipice.

Cost containment. Another factor in debates over health care and treatment strategies is the issue of cost. It is tremendously expensive to provide the state-of-the-art benefits a modern hospital offers. Concerns about where the money will come from to care for a fast-growing population of elderly citizens appear to be making the case for active "mercy killing" even more compelling.

Between 1960 and 1984, the United States has seen a 1000 percent increase in health expenditures. In 1960, Americans spent about $129 per person on health care. By 1984, we were paying $1,500 per person.[12] In 1987, Dr. Howard H. Hiatt estimated the cost per person at more than $2,000.[13] Approximately two-thirds of these costs are now paid by the government or private insurance companies.[14]

Several factors have contributed to this phenomenal upsurge in cost. New technologies such as kidney dialysis became available. More Americans had access to institutional health care as their incomes rose. And more and more employers paid for health insurance benefits to cover their workers. The longer life spans of most Americans, adding to a growing population of elderly citizens, has increased costs as well. Hiatt notes that when today's ten-year-olds turn sixty-five, they and the rest of the elderly will require 45 percent of the health dollars spent in America, compared with 30 percent today.[15]

Government-funded research into important diseases has sped the development of new techniques. In turn, public demand for access to new procedures—and physicians eager to try them—continues to fuel a health-care price spiral. Fear among doctors that they may face malpractice lawsuits keeps their costs high. Specialists, such as surgeons, obstetricians, and radiologists, may pay malpractice premiums exceeding $25,000 per year.[16]

The results of these realities, some physicians say, is that we are rationing medical care by default. The demand for heart transplants, for example, vastly exceeds the supply of usable hearts from accident victims or other likely donors.[17] What does this mean for elderly Americans, and what does it have to do with our discussion on euthanasia? Judith Wilson Ross and William Winslade, in their book *Choosing Life or Death: A Guide for Patients, Families and Professionals*, explain what is happening:

> Newspapers are now reporting that seriously ill elderly patients are being moved on to nursing homes—moves that result in earlier deaths—when the costs of their treatment exceed what will be reimbursed through Medicare. Hospitals may cut back on services to those people without political power as a form of cost-saving. . . . The rationing that is currently being attempted is the worst kind, for it is chaotic and hidden and probably reaches most quickly to those who are most vulnerable and least powerful. It elevates the preferences of the wealthy and affluent to moral values and reduces the very lives and well-being of the less affluent and the poor to matters of indifference. And it permits us to deny what we are doing.[18]

How It Started: The Kidney Dialysis Story

The development of bioethics began in the 1960s as health-care professionals realized that the revolution in new medical technology called for clear ethical guidelines. One of the major developments leading up to this was the kidney dialysis machine. Kidneys remove impurities from the blood, and if a person's kidneys fail, he gradually becomes poisoned by his own bodily wastes and dies.

In 1960, Dr. Belding Scribner made a discovery that provided new life and new hope to victims of kidney disease. He invented a shunt which can be implanted in a patient's vein and used repeatedly for dialysis, or machine cleansing of the blood. Before the shunt, dialysis required direct access to the patient's veins; when his veins were used up, no other option was available.

As reliable, long-term dialysis became a reality, doctors were faced with a new frustration. Sometimes no machine was available for their patient, or a patient simply could not afford the prolonged expense of treatment for kidney failure. Between 1962 and 1972, hospital selection committees performed the gruesome task of selecting some kidney patients to live, and some to die.

A clamor in the U. S. Congress finally forced the issue, as patients and their families demanded federal support for equitable provision of dialysis. In 1972, an amendment to Medicare became law. It extended Medicare coverage to every patient under age sixty-five who needed kidney dialysis. The government's projections at the time suggested that dialysis would be needed for no more than twenty thousand patients. But by 1980, three times that number were receiving dialysis paid for by Medicare. An expected $75 million expense per year has reached $1.2 billion annually, burdening Medicare significantly.[19]

The scarcity of available dialysis treatment in the early 1960s changed radically. As kidney dialysis became widely available, "anyone in kidney failure was promptly placed on dialysis, regardless of medical prognosis," according to Ross and Winslade. "Families began to beg that patients not be given dialysis, though these requests were seldom honored, whether they came from the family or the patients themselves."[20]

A poignant example of how this is forcing us to come to grips with decisions regarding treatment comes from U. S. Surgeon General C. Everett Koop. He wrote in *Christianity Today* about his mother's death from uterine cancer at age eighty-seven. "She was in a coma, during which people actually asked me if I wanted to put her on dialysis. That would have been ridiculous for personal, spiritual, and economic reasons." Koop went on to speculate about a similar choice that might someday confront him directly. "If my kidney shut down tomorrow, let's say, after a severe infection, I don't know how long I would want to be on dialysis. It would be foolish and a waste of resources for me to have a kidney transplant at my age. I would probably opt to clean up my affairs, say good-bye to my family, and drift out in uremia."[21]

The Wild Card: AIDS

Decisions involving kidney dialysis for elderly patients are undeniably difficult, but they pale in comparison with choices confronting individuals and society concerning a new health threat: Acquired Immune Deficiency Syndrome, or AIDS. In the face of a growing AIDS epidemic, medical experts, policy makers, and families will face unimagined challenges that involve all the factors we have discussed: medical research and technique, cost, and the anguish of weighing individual health care needs against the need to protect and provide for society at large.

AIDS is confronting the medical profession with something new: a relatively young population of terminally ill patients. What constitutes wise and compassionate treatment for people with a ravaging disease that is, so far, 100 percent fatal? Many doctors and ethicists believe AIDS will be a watershed indicator of society's willingness to tolerate euthanasia, if alternatives are not developed quickly.

At the same time, there may be some positive developments from the tragedy of AIDS. Doctors may have to resume the role MacGregor described earlier, that of guiding the patient through his disease rather than combating it on all fronts. Also, our ability as a society to talk about death and dying and to come to terms with it more openly may be enhanced. And new possibilities for home care or hospice care for the dying may, out of necessity, be developed.

At MacGregor's hospital in Philadelphia, AIDS patients are often referred to his division for tertiary care. In a recent instance, MacGregor illustrates how the goal of treatment differs for such a terminal patient. A laborer in his early thirties, married and with two children, contracted AIDS when he shared an intravenous needle for illegal drug use. He came to MacGregor with pneumocystic pneumonia, was treated for it, and responded well. He went back to work but contracted the same type of pneumonia six months later. MacGregor's goal each time he treated him was "to stabilize him and get him home as soon as I could."

Finally, the patient suffered a stroke and lesions were found on his brain. If he had not had AIDS, MacGregor said, the standard procedure would be to operate and perform a biopsy to see if the lesions were cancerous. MacGregor chose not to intervene so aggressively; he treated the patient with drugs for the most likely cause of the brain lesions. That way the patient was able to return home to his family, although he was too weak to work. After several weeks, his wife called MacGregor to report that her husband was having difficulty breathing. MacGregor said, "You can bring him in if you want to. It's up to you." The wife replied that she thought death was imminent, so she chose to keep him at home. "He died that night," MacGregor said, "and I believe that keeping him home was the right thing to do."[22]

Surgeon General Koop says we are rapidly approaching an important decision point regarding AIDS treatment:

> By the year 1991, AIDS will affect enough people so that 54,000 will die. At the present time, AIDS patients are in intensive care beds for as long as they have insurance, and then they are put in acute care beds. We are probably taking care of AIDS the wrong way now, and we can't continue to do so much longer. AIDS patients really belong in a hospice system, kept at home with minimal assistance while they are still independent, and then brought

into a shelter where all they need is a roof, a bed, warmth, food, and tender loving care. They do not need high-tech assistance.

In view of available resources, Koop maintains, "we're going to have to face that issue soon."

Choosing not to treat a terminal patient vigorously is clearly different from euthanasia. MacGregor insists that doctors need to sharpen their discernment of when death is imminent and resolve to step back at that point and allow it to happen. This is necessitated by the array of options medical science presents today, and it will not be easy. The line between choosing not to treat and actively causing the death of a patient grows extremely fuzzy at times. A further complication is the well-organized pressure to allow assisted suicide and direct euthanasia.

The Debate over Withholding Food and Water

Treatment decisions that concern the withdrawal of artificially provided food and water affect many thousands more patients than the present number of AIDS sufferers. It is on this point that a serious debate is being waged today; the line between "allowing" death and "assisting" it often grows obscure.

Providing food and water to a patient, even if it is dripped into his body through a tube, has powerful symbolic significance in our society. "For I was hungry and you gave me something to eat, I was thirsty and you gave me something to drink," Jesus says in Matthew 25:35. Those simple responses to basic human needs are widely perceived as fundamental requirements of human compassion. Could there ever be an occasion where it is not appropriate to provide food and water to a person who cannot nourish himself? This extremely challenging question would never have occurred to nurses and physicians in an age before medical technology developed ways to feed unconscious, incapacitated people and to bypass failing stomachs and mouths. Doctors are being faced, once again, with choices they are often ethically unprepared to make. Sometimes those decisions appear terribly wrong.

The case of Baby Doe in Bloomington, Indiana, brought the issue of depriving patients of food and water to the forefront of national consciousness in 1982. Decisions to deny treatment or care to handicapped or damaged infants have been documented for years, but the Indiana situation gained far more media attention. Causing a handicapped infant to die, at the request of the parents or on the advice of a doctor, has been viewed as ethically more acceptable than terminating the life of an adult. It is a logical extension of the abortion mentality that has undermined the value of unborn life since 1973.

For some reason, however, seeing Baby Doe die of starvation captured the imagination of the American public and provoked considerable outrage. Baby Doe was born with Down's Syndrome, which produces varying levels of mental retardation. Baby Doe also had a blocked esophagus, preventing the food he swallowed from reaching his stomach. His esophageal deformity was a condition that could be corrected readily with surgery. His parents refused to allow the operation or intravenous feeding, so pediatricians at the hospital petitioned the courts for an order for life-saving treatment. The Indiana State Supreme Court refused. In six days, Baby Doe was dead.

Later, the landmark case of Claire Conroy (see chapter 3) raised the same issue with regard to a severely impaired elderly patient. Are the doctors who withdraw food and water from patients committing the moral equivalent of murder? Courts have said no, but there are no explicit regulations preventing them from deciding otherwise. In 1986, the American Medical Association (AMA) published guidelines on the issue, identifying artificial nutrition and hydration as treatment procedures that could ethically be withheld from a patient in an irreversible coma. They found it to be similar to decisions, widely accepted in the medical community, to stop using a respirator to keep a patient breathing. It is clear, however, that a patient could conceivably breathe on his own once a respirator is turned off, as Karen Quinlan did for ten years before she died. When nourishment is withdrawn from a patient who cannot feed himself, death is imminent and unavoidable.

There are three major ways in which nutrition and hydration are provided to patients. First, gastronomy involves surgically inserting a tube into the stomach. Second, intravenous fluids enter the body from a needle directly into the veins. Finally, the most widely available technique is the nasogastric tube. The tube is inserted through the patient's nose, pushed down the back of his throat and through his esophagus into his stomach. It can be extremely irritating and hazardous, triggering vomiting and bleeding.[23]

Guidelines for Nontreatment

In 1984, the Society for Health and Human Values held a conference in Philadelphia. A wide range of views on withholding or withdrawing food and water was presented, and the papers from the conference were published in a book, *By No Extraordinary Means: The Choice to Forgo Life-Sustaining Food and Water*, edited by Dr. Joanne Lynn. The arguments presented in this book and the cautious conclusion drawn by Lynn provide a foundation for understanding the debate and responding to it from a Christian worldview.

Lynn, an associate professor of geriatric medicine at George Washington University Medical Center, and James F. Childress, professor of religious studies and medical education at the University of Virginia, outline the following possible situations in which offering a patient food and water is not essential:

When treatment is futile. They illustrate this with an example of a patient with a severe body burn whose blood will not clot adequately. Physically, it would be extremely difficult and painful to hook up the patient to any form of artificial feeding. In other instances where death is imminent no matter what treatment is given, Lynn and Childress suggest that feeding is not necessary.

When there is no possible benefit for the patient. If a patient has lost consciousness permanently, his family and care-givers may become convinced that artificial feeding is "offensive and unreasonable." That, they say, should be sufficient reason to decide to withhold nourishment.

When artificial feeding presents a disproportionate burden. If a severely demented patient, for instance, required restraints in order to receive food and water artificially, the process could become a source of fear and struggle. Lynn and Childress write, "a decision not to intervene, except perhaps briefly to ascertain that there are no treatable causes, might allow such a patient to live out a shorter life with fair freedom of movement and freedom from fear, while a decision to maintain artificial nutrition and hydration might consign the patient to end his or her life in unremitting anguish."[24]

A different perspective is presented by Daniel Callahan, director of the Hastings Center in New York. He points out that "if the practice of ceasing to feed some dying patients would remain as rare" as the handful of cases allowed by Lynn and Childress, "the matter need be of little public interest." However, he cautions that due to the pressure to reduce costs and the frustrations felt by doctors in long-term or chronic care facilities, growing enthusiasm for withholding food and water is apparent.

In the future, because of trends in aging and the likelihood that good health in old age will give way to chronic disorders, Callahan argues that many lives will be at stake. There are several factors he identifies as counterweights to decisions to withhold food and water. These include:

The "klutz" factor. What might happen, he wonders, if caregivers in the future "withhold food and water thoughtlessly, carelessly, and incorrectly, thereby causing much suffering. . . ?"

The scandal factor. If it appears to the media or to the community at large that hospitals are basing their treatment withdrawal choices on the basis of race, "quality of life," or other subjective factors, the results for the medical community could be devastating.

Making it mandatory. Finally, matters of choice often become requirements of law. Because of economic and other social pressures, the same could happen regarding withholding food and water. "To curtail moral damage in the future," Callahan writes, "I think we must begin now to draw the lines very carefully."[25]

Professors Alan J. Weisbard and Mark Siegler represent the most cautious position on forgoing nutrition and hydration. They appeal for a prohibition on actions to withhold food and water, arguing that starvation and dehydration rather than the illness itself become the cause of death in some of these patients. Because of this distinction, removing food and water is significantly different from turning off a respirator or stopping kidney dialysis so that nature can take its course.

Also, in the current environment of concern over cost and a growing elderly population, these two professors believe "it may well prove convenient—and all too easy—to move from recognition of an individual's 'right to die'. . . to a climate enforcing a socially obligatory duty to die.'" Weisbard and Siegler acknowledge that their concern stems more from apprehension about the impact of such decisions on attitudes in society than concern about any particular patient and his family.

They conclude that "the compassionate call for withdrawing or withholding fluids and nutrition in a few, selected cases bears the seeds of great potential abuse." As an alternative to withdrawing food or water, they suggest that society and the medical profession channel its energies toward improving the comfort and quality of life for patients who must rely on artificial feeding and hydration.[26]

Conclusion

Ethicists and physicians are groping for answers to urgent questions posed by modern medical technique. The debate is very much alive, and the direction it will take during future decades as America grows old is yet unknown. Certainly the debate has been joined from all sides. As Christians in America begin to consider ministry to elderly believers and the choices and challenges facing an aging church, they need to have a firm grasp on all aspects of this debate.

In chapter 2, we will explore some of the voices influencing popular opinion on the "right to die" and the development of public policy in Holland that tolerates euthanasia. Will America move in the same direction, perhaps before we know it? That is the question we will examine next.

Chapter 1, Notes

1. Gridiron Club annual dinner, March 1987, cited in the *Washington Post* health section, 14 April 1987.

2. Department of Commerce, Bureau of the Census, *Demographic and Socioeconomic Aspects of Aging in the United States, Current Population Reports*, August 1984, 5.

3. Ibid.

4. Ibid., 17.

5. Ibid., 48.

6. Department of Commerce, Bureau of the Census, *Age Structure of the U.S. Population in the 21st Century, Statistical Brief*, December 1986.

7. Howard H. Hiatt, M. D., *America's Health in the Balance: Choice or Chance?* (New York: Harper and Row, 1987), 53.

8. Ibid.

9. Ibid., 49.

10. Interview with Dr. Rob Roy MacGregor, 5 June 1987.

11. Rob Roy MacGregor, "The Inevitability of Death," *Christianity Today*, 6 March 1987, 24.

12. Judith Wilson Ross and William J. Winslade, *Choosing Life or Death: A Guide for Patients, Families and Professionals* (New York: The Free Press, 1986), 12.

13. Hiatt, *America's Health*, 3.

14. Ross and Winslade, *Choosing Life or Death*, 12-13.

15. Hiatt, *America's Health*, 6.

16. Ibid., 32.

17. Ross and Winslade, *Choosing Life or Death*, 70.

18. Ibid., 20-21.

19. Ibid.

20. Ibid.

21. C. Everett Koop, "The End Is Not the End," *Christianity Today*, 6 March 1987, 18.

22. MacGregor interview.

23. David Major, M. D., "The Medical Procedures for Providing Food and Water: Indications and Effects" in *By No Extraordinary Means: The Choice to Forgo Life-Sustaining Food and Water*, ed. Joanne Lynn, M. D.(Bloomington, Ind.: Indiana University Press, 1986), 25.

24. Joanne Lynn and James F. Childress, "Must Patients Always Be Given Food and Water?" in *By No Extraordinary Means*, 51, 52, 53.

25. Daniel Callahan, "Public Policy and the Cessation of Nutrition," in *By No Extraordinary Means*, 63-66.

26. Alan J. Weisbard and Mark Siegler, "On Killing Patients with Kindness: An Appeal for Caution," in *By No Extraordinary Means, 114-15*.

Chapter 2

The Power of Persuasion:
The Influence of Medical Realities on Societal Attitudes

You are a member of the first generation of doctors in the history of medicine to turn their backs on the oath of Hippocrates and kill millions of old useless people, unborn children, born malformed children, for the good of mankind—and to do so without a single murmur from one of you.

That outburst comes from an addled old priest in Walker Percy's acclaimed novel, *The Thanatos Syndrome*. Father Smith, at the brink of having his hospice ministry taken away from him, gives a bewildered psychiatrist a piece of his mind. "Do you know what is going to happen to you?" he queries. "You're going to end up killing Jews."[1]

Set in a future America where infants may be put to death before they attain their "legal rights" at age eighteen months, *The Thanatos Syndrome* offers a gripping apologetic for life. Author Percy details in chilling terms the unforeseen results of manipulating and meddling with human nature to suit the whims of technocratic doctors. For the sake of achieving high-minded social goals—from reducing crime to producing winning football teams—doctors in this brave new America rationalize a devious way to alter the brain chemistry of unsuspecting residents of rural Louisiana.

THE BATTLE FOR PUBLIC OPINION

Mass Market Commentary

The Thanatos Syndrome is remarkable because it is a lone voice in the wilderness of American fiction, docudrama, and news reporting that portray euthanasia sympathetically, tugging at heartstrings with tales of suffering. Percy provides a powerful counterweight to other recent examples of mass market commentary on the "right to die," such as:

- Betty Rollin's book *Last Wish*, the true account of how she assisted her ailing mother to commit suicide (described previously in the Introduction).

- A made-for-television movie, *Baby Girl Scott*, depicting the anguish of parents with a premature, handicapped infant. In *Baby Girl Scott*, the doctors caring for the baby are portrayed as callously indifferent to human suffering. They verge on viewing the baby as a ready-made guinea pig for experimental, high-tech treatment.

- *This Far and No More*, a true story by Andrew H. Malcolm about a forty-year-old woman who developed amyotrophic lateral sclerosis (Lou Gehrig's disease). Frustrated and horrified at her progressive inability to move, and finally even to speak or nod, Emily Bauer decides she wants to die. Her husband contacts a group called Concern for Dying, and with legal assistance they accomplish their goal.

- *Mercy or Murder*, a television dramatization about Roswell Gilbert, who shot his wife in 1985 to end her suffering from Alzheimer's disease. Gilbert was found guilty of first-degree murder. But the television version of this true event ends with Gilbert, portrayed by actor Robert Young (best known for his role as Marcus Welby, M. D.), urging that euthanasia be legalized.

With the exception of *Baby Girl Scott*, these popular media interpretations of the right to die neglect solutions other than assisted suicide. In *Last Wish*, Rollin's mother experiences prolonged, intractable pain. Emily Bauer finds herself tragically alienated from her two daughters, who cannot ever remember seeing their mother walk. These are indeed terrible situations that call for abundant love and sacrifice in response. But the cry for assisted suicide emanating from each begs several important questions: Why did Rollin not spend her energies lobbying for better pain control for her mother? Why were these suicide wishes accepted almost unconditionally, without reference to the tragedy of broken relationships? In most instances, the desire for suicide indicates depression and a cry for help. Why was it not treated that way—at least initially—in these cases?

Beyond the questions of what these individuals really needed, these examples fail to consider broader implications for society. If public policy is based on emotion-laden cases like these, how will our fundamental view of the value of life change? That concern apparently does not cross the minds of these authors and artists. Joseph J. Piccione, author of a monograph on medical ethics, warns us what the ultimate result may be:

> Modern psychology tells us that when a person in deep distress talks about suicide, it is really a cry for help and for care. When this cry comes to the ears of a society which affirms the goodness of life at all stages, the response is to control the pain and to be present and to love the person. When a society changes to a utilitarian view of life, to an ultimate kind of consumerism in which life is possessed until it is no longer enjoyable, then the cry for death will be taken at face value.[2]

Failing to consider alternatives for patients in deep need of care and comfort—even when they request death—can become habitual. We grow so accustomed to hearing about the hard cases, the heart-rending stories, that we gradually begin to believe there is a place in our social order for physicians to take the lives of their patients. In chapter 9, we will consider a leading alternative for the terminally ill: the hospice movement. "Hospice" is a concept, not a place, and it is seen as a promising way to make euthanasia not only unacceptable but irrelevant. Public consensus in this country has a long way to go, however, before that is accomplished.

Where Fact Meets Fiction

Popular media can be instrumental in shaping public attitudes, particularly when true stories of heart-rending hard cases are reported. The impact of the case of Karen Ann Quinlan, mentioned briefly in the preceding chapter, probably shifted American public awareness and sympathy about patients' rights more than any other. Ironically, her family and parish priest, who was instrumental in helping the family decide to end artificial respiration, had no interest whatsoever in promoting the cause of euthanasia.

Karen Ann Quinlan lapsed into a coma at age twenty-one after taking a combination of pills and drinking gin and tonic. She suffered irreversible brain damage and was placed on life support in a New Jersey hospital. Her parents, in consultation with their priest, sought a court order to turn the respirator off. Initially their request was denied, but in a landmark 1976 decision, the New Jersey Supreme Court granted permission. Karen Ann surprised everyone by remaining alive, though permanently unconscious, until 1985.

Following the Quinlan experience, there has been a marked increase in public acceptance of the idea that a physician should "help" his terminally ill patient to die. A Roper poll, commissioned by the pro-euthanasia Hemlock Society in 1986, found 62 percent responding "yes" when asked "whether or not doctors should be allowed by law to end the life of a suffering terminally ill patient if the patient requests it."[3] Only 27 percent said "no" and 10 percent had no answer or did not know. A 1983 poll by the National Opinion Research Center found a 63 percent positive response to a similar question. That figure was up from a 44 percent approval rate in 1947 and 36 percent approval in 1950.[4]

Results like these may reflect a combination of influences on American public opinion, including the sway that popular books and movies hold over the imagination. Opinion favoring euthanasia also underscores the inroads made by proponents of the right to die. While books and movies work their charm on the population at large, advocates of "death with dignity" are sharpening their skills of persuasion among professionals in medicine, law, and ethics.

Right-to-Die Proponents

The premiere example of this is Joseph Fletcher, an Episcopal priest who established the New York-based Society for the Right to Die. Fletcher is best known for his defense of situation ethics, opposing the view that objective standards of right and wrong ought to guide human behavior. In his book *Humanhood: Essays in Biomedical Ethics*, Fletcher vigorously promotes his pro-euthanasia view. "It is harder morally to justify letting somebody die a slow and ugly death, dehumanized," he writes, "than it is to justify helping him to escape from such misery."[5]

Fletcher, whose ethical reasoning will be explored more fully in chapter 4, blurs distinctions between treatment choices and active death promotion. He argues,

> The plain fact is that indirect or negative euthanasia is already a fait accompli in modern medicine. Every day in a hundred hospitals across the land, decisions are made clinically that the line has been crossed from prolonging genuinely human life to only prolonging subhuman dying; and when that judgment is made, respirators are turned off, life-perpetuating

intravenous infusions stopped, proposed surgery canceled, and drugs countermanded.[6]

All of this is true, as we saw in chapter 1. But this need not be euthanasia, or even a qualified "negative euthanasia," as Fletcher claims. The critical difference is whether the focus is on the patient himself or the treatment in question. Fletcher would have physicians base decisions on the patient's "quality of life." This murky concept, rooted in the relativity of situation ethics, puts the doctor in the driver's seat with near total command of what happens to the patient. Since the doctor in this case intends for the patient to die, Fletcher points out that it scarcely matters whether death comes because the doctor actively induces it or merely omits treatment.

In fact, Fletcher says of the idea of letting the patient go, "this euthanasia practice is manifestly superficial, morally timid, and evasive of the real issue." Better to end it quickly, he suggests, with a painless injection.[7]

Ethicists who reject Fletcher's reasoning draw a firm distinction between correct treatment choices and active assistance in dying. In other words, a physician may opt to end chemotherapy or even withdraw a respirator when that particular treatment is no longer useful to the patient. The patient may die, but the physician does not intend to hasten death. More importantly, the doctor in this instance is making no judgment about the patient's quality of life. He is confining his role to the realm of medical treatment and not using an arbitrary set of criteria about what makes life worth living.

This point of view is essentially endorsed by the Roman Catholic church as well as Protestant ethicists who reject "quality of life" considerations and instead value the sanctity of life. "Catholic morality allows one to judge the benefits and burdens of different treatments, not the value or quality of individual human lives," writes Richard Doerflinger of the National Council of Catholic Bishops' Office for Pro-Life Activities.[8]

Rather than blur distinctions, as Fletcher does, Doerflinger carefully reasons that withdrawing life-sustaining treatment may or may not be the moral equivalent of euthanasia. "When treatment seems useless or unduly burdensome, the church refers to it as 'extraordinary' and recognizes that a patient may choose to accept or refuse it."[9]

By defining euthanasia broadly, including in its scope even routine, accepted decisions for ending treatment, Fletcher appeals to common sense and compassion as he promotes all sorts of euthanasia practices. He is joined by proponents of assisted suicide who have formed the Hemlock Society, an organization working to pass laws in various states to legalize the practice.

Other Influences in American Culture

As right-to-die advocates and popular media sound the same drumbeat for euthanasia, they are assisted by other pervasive realities in current American culture. Three influences in particular offer ready-made reasons euthanasia may be gaining substantial ground in the battle for public opinion.

"It's not so different from abortion." It is no coincidence that some of the most ardent euthanasia opponents come from the prolife movement. The parallels are many. Before abortion was legalized by the U. S. Supreme Court in 1973, women obtained back-alley, illegal abortions. Often they were tragically maimed or killed, and these "horror stories" formed the basis of a movement to change the law. These stories are like today's "hard cases," where illegal assisted suicide (as in the case of Betty Rollin and her mother) becomes a legendary source of motivation for rallying ordinary people to the cause.

Advocates of both abortion and euthanasia anchor their positions in what they call "a right to privacy." The individual, in other words, has (or should have) complete autonomy over his or her body. Unborn babies, according to some abortion proponents, are not persons so they have no rights. Similarly, Joseph Fletcher has redefined "personhood" to exclude some terminally ill or incapacitated individuals. Fletcher notes, "If we are morally obliged to put an end to a pregnancy when an amniocentesis reveals a terribly defective fetus, we are equally obliged to put an end to a patient's hopeless misery when a brain scan reveals that a patient with cancer has advanced brain metastases."[10]

Of course, most of today's 1.5 million abortions each year in the United States are done for the mother's convenience, and many aborted fetuses are completely normal developing children. Our society's tolerance for abortion quickly accommodated not only the few desperate women who sought the back-alley doctors but also millions of women relying on abortion as an alternative to birth control.

The same slide down a slippery slope with regard to euthanasia is not difficult to imagine. If a comatose cancer patient is deemed a nonperson today, what will keep society from expanding the definition as health care costs and a population squeeze become increasingly intolerable? When will we reach the point of performing so-called mercy killings primarily for our convenience rather than the patient's presumed comfort?

It may be far more difficult in the long run to battle euthanasia than abortion, because the victim may seem willing, not defenseless. Euthanasia is not accomplished by violent means, such as saline abortion (which burns the fetus alive) or dismemberment. And the fact that most candidates for euthanasia have lived out their lives makes the option for death seem more palatable than it is for an infant just getting a start in life.

Surgeon General C. Everett Koop notes with alarm that the Christian community was slow and uncoordinated in its initial response to abortion on demand. He says bluntly, "The Christian public was caught napping by abortion and infanticide. It took 12 years for the number of crisis pregnancy centers to equal the number of abortion clinics. Here we are at the threshold of euthanasia, and my plea is, 'Let's move faster than we did with abortion.'"

"Elderly people who are terminally ill have a duty to die and get out of the way." This quote came from Colorado governor Richard D. Lamm in 1984 in an address to the Colorado

Health Lawyers Association.[11] It provides palpable evidence of how rapidly society's perception of an individual's "right to die" can deteriorate into a utilitarian "duty to die." Apparently no vestige of a sanctity-of-life perspective pricked the conscience of this middle-aged politician.

Lamm's comments reflect an accurate picture of how society—all of us—may begin thinking about euthanasia as people such as Fletcher keep up a steady drumbeat of persuasion, pushing just a little at a time toward general acceptance of all-out mercy killing. This is serious enough, but Lamm's words carry a subtler message—and one that may hit even closer to home: a built-in bias against the elderly. Evangelical sociologist David Moberg laments age discrimination, which he describes as a belief that the elderly have "lost their creativity, can no longer contribute to productive goals in society, cannot change and grow, and that they live in the past."

The elderly do experience real losses—loss of hearing, vision, mobility, energy, strength, income, and friends and family members who begin dying off. Even at church, Moberg says, a sense of loss can be perpetuated. "Often, leadership positions are declared off limits," he says. "At the very time when many older people have more time on their hands to give, the culture in which they find themselves decrees they're not qualified for election to church offices."

The reasons for ageism are varied. They include cultural ideals that America, as a "young" nation, has always cherished: youth, beauty, energy, vigor, and good health. Old age is a reminder of our mortality and frailty and the inevitable changes in life that we delay facing for as long as possible.

Another reason behind prejudice against the elderly is fragmentation in the family. Fewer extended family members live near one another today. The generations do not mingle much, so the elderly in our midst run a substantial risk of winding up as isolated strangers.

There are some positive signs that this is changing. Because of the "squaring of the pyramid" discussed in chapter 1, there will soon be more elderly people in America than ever before. Meanwhile, younger age groups are dwindling in size. In some areas of the country, the impact of these population shifts are already apparent in the workplace. In Washington, D. C., developers of suburban hotels are recruiting among nursing home residents for employees. McDonald's restaurants pitch employment ads to the senior set. And senior citizen associations such as the American Association for Retired Persons project images of old age that accent variety, enthusiasm for living, and continued productivity. A book by former president Jimmy Carter and his wife, *Everything to Gain: Making the Most of the Rest of Your Life* (Random House, 1987), gives a first-hand account of ways to preserve physical and mental stamina after retirement.

For the Christian community, Moberg suggests recapturing the import of the commandment, "Honor your father and mother." What does that require? "To honor the elderly does not mean confining them to rocking chairs in the pattern of Whistler's Mother. Nor does it mean obeying them just as long as one is a child," Moberg says. "But in the biblical context of ancient Israel, to honor meant to pay attention to commands, wishes, and advice. To care for people in time of need. To cope with their faults. And eventually to experience oneself the honor in righteousness of becoming an elder person."

"As long as you have your health, you have everything." This bit of home-spun philosophy reflects the high priority Americans, in particular, place on health, wholeness, and fitness. Those are magnificent blessings, but they are not guaranteed. As medical abilities have grown more and more sophisticated, our response as a society has been to take advanced medical care and treatment increasingly for granted. This is borne out not only by how we, as individuals, interact with physicians and health-care institutions, but in public policy debates as well.

Ethicist Judith Wilson Ross notes, "After World War II, the U. S. government became the major financial backer of medical research." Basic knowledge advanced rapidly, and so did public demand for access to new treatments, usually at someone else's expense (either insurance companies or from public funding). "In time," Ross writes, "virtually every disease had its lobby and its congressional spokesperson, urging increased funding."[12]

A new mindset has arisen, a mindset Surgeon General Koop says is apparent in the very terminology of the modern medical marketplace: the patient is called a consumer "as though he were eating cereal," and the physician is called a provider "as though he were delivering gasoline." When patients and their families approach medical care from this point of view, Koop maintains, they tend to expect nothing less than total success. But "human bodies are not like carburetors: the same thing does not affect all patients in the same way," Koop writes. "There is an inherent failure rate in all that the physician seeks to accomplish."[13]

An inability to cure, then, is seen as a defeat rather than an opportunity for alternative types of care. And what shall we do with the objects of our failure? It seems all too likely that the logical response may be to dispose of them.

When we allow ourselves to believe that "good health is everything," we are forced to swallow as well the idea that the loss of health is nothing short of disastrous—the end of the line. Christians know that this frame of reference has little in common with biblical truth.

At issue, fundamentally, are questions of control and autonomy. We want to be in charge of every aspect of our lives, particularly our physical well-being. This attitude is reinforced by court decisions regarding life and death, as chapter 3 will demonstrate. Where, in all of this, is our sense of God's sovereignty? Will we, even as Christians, be pressed into society's mold of thinking health is the necessary prerequisite for human happiness and fulfillment? If so, we aid and abet the pro-euthanasia advocates by embracing their most basic premise: equating human value and physical well-being.

Euthanasia in Holland: A Case Study

Various forces at work in society, such as population trends, ageism, soaring medical costs, and a presumed "right of privacy," may be combining to make euthanasia more acceptable here in the United States. In the Netherlands, that process has advanced well beyond the current debate in America. Like the rest of western Europe, the "squaring of the pyramid" in Holland is about one generation, or forty years, ahead of the United States. The proportion of elderly people in the population as a whole is growing significantly faster than other age groups.

Partly as a result of this, euthanasia is practiced regularly there, and not just the "passive" variety in which a physician "lets go" of a dying patient. Instead, physicians are reported to provide lethal injections for patients who request them. Estimates of the number of assisted deaths range from five thousand per year to as many as twelve thousand, or 10 percent of the deaths each year.

Active euthanasia remains technically illegal. However, court decisions since 1973 have made it possible for physicians to successfully plead "mercy killing" as a defense when they are charged with causing or assisting the death of a patient. The subject provokes deep controversy in Holland, and both sides of the debate acknowledge the nation is pioneering a social solution with little idea of where it is ultimately headed.

Alan L. Otten, a reporter for the *Wall Street Journal*, notes in a story from Amsterdam, "the Netherlands may be the laboratory to determine whether active euthanasia can be employed with circumspection to provide 'death with dignity' for people in extreme suffering or whether once a foot is placed on this slippery slope, a descent into wholesale slaughter becomes almost inevitable."[14]

Death by Request

Dutch law still views active euthanasia as murder, punishable by up to twelve years in prison. One doctor, P. L. S.

Schoonheim, was brought to trial in 1983 for providing a lethal injection for a ninety-five-year-old woman who requested "death with dignity." She refused to have a hip fracture repaired and became an invalid. Schoonheim and a medical colleague interviewed her several times to be certain she knew exactly what she was requesting. Convinced of her sincerity and of their own inability to treat her, they essentially "put her to sleep" with lethal injections.

Schoonheim was found guilty, but on appeal the Supreme Court of the Netherlands disagreed with the lower court's ruling. The high court ordered the lower court to determine whether his action was in accord with "an objective medical view." The lower court said an objective medical view was not possible, but substituted "a reasonable medical view" as a measure of the act's legitimacy. After four years, Schoonheim was acquitted.[15]

This is significant because it essentially leaves to physicians the task of determining whether euthanasia should be done. As long as physicians act within the boundaries of guidelines determined by the courts, their plea of "mercy killing" generally frees them from criminal charges. The criteria are:

- The patient must be experiencing intolerable and insufferable physical or psychological torment.
- The patient's suffering and his desire to die must persist.
- Deciding to die must be a voluntary act of the patient alone.
- The patient must comprehend his situation and weigh the alternatives.
- No other reasonable solution to the patient's dilemma is apparent.
- The decision to assist a patient to die cannot be made by just one person.
- A physician who is responsible for prescribing a lethal dose of medication must be present.

- No unnecessary suffering may be brought upon others by the decision.[16]

These criteria were adopted in 1987 by the Royal Dutch Medical Association, and a commission appointed by the Dutch government reached similar conclusions. In political circles, pressure to formally acknowledge similar criteria—and thus make euthanasia truly legal—became intense. The Liberal Party introduced legislation to move Holland toward legalization, and the Christian Democrats, traditionally opposed to changing the law, put forward a bill in which euthanasia hinges on the concrete expectation or anticipation of death.

The bills, according to opponents of euthanasia in the Netherlands, differ only in degree. In an "appeal to fellow citizens," three leading Christian professors wrote, "Will the government protect the lives of citizens except from physicians? Will physicians be free from criminal charges and penalties as they kill within legal limits?"[17]

A morass of problems emerging out of the established criteria causes some to reject the idea completely. For example, some pro-euthanasia forces in Holland argue for the classification of comatose patients as candidates for eventual euthanasia, even though the condition of these patients does not begin to meet the nationally accepted criteria protecting physicians from prosecution. They are not terminal, they cannot make treatment decisions for themselves, and they likely do not suffer "intolerable" pain.

The three professors write, "How free can people be who request euthanasia? A sick person in a terminal situation, in our view, is not free. Therefore we reject such decisions. Such people are dependent on others. This dependence makes an illusion of the decision for euthanasia being a 'free' one."

Building Grass-Roots Support
While attempts at formalizing euthanasia attract headlines and controversy, a voluntary organization is quietly building public support in favor of euthanasia. The Dutch Association

for Voluntary Euthanasia, begun in 1973, "aims at the social acceptance of voluntary euthanasia in our country and ultimately also at legalization."[18] The organization has twenty-six thousand dues-paying members, publishes a quarterly magazine, and boasts a professionally managed "members' aid service." This "service" offers medical advice, information kits, and lecturers on the subject. Jeane Tromp Meesters, coordinator for the group, notes that about 650 clients each year come to the members' aid service for advice on how to cope with a terminally ill patient who is requesting death. Trained volunteers style themselves as "andragologists"—people who offer guidance to others who "wish to change in a self-chosen direction."[19]

The volunteers arrange a meeting with the patient to make certain the death wish is genuine and not imposed by relatives or others. They attempt to assess the patient's communication with his doctor, the level of pain relief, and his actual awareness of what a death request means. In an article about the member's aid service, Meesters writes, "Approximately a third of our clients are incurably ill, although not all of them in a terminal stage. Many of them suffer from cancer. One-fifth of the demands for help come from old to very old people who suffer from different kinds of old-age ailments such as loneliness, isolation, or the feeling that they have lived long enough."

When the group is approached by relatives on behalf of a permanently unconscious patient, Meesters notes, "the relatives have no right to ask for euthanasia. . . . In cases like these, the only thing we can advise is to plead with the doctors not to continue senseless medical treatment." The organization supports withdrawal of artificially administered food and water: "Dying through starvation and/or dehydration need not be as horrible as doctors and nurses are led to believe, especially with terminal patients who do not want to eat or drink anymore themselves."[20]

Results of surveys in the Netherlands reveal the inroads this group has achieved in influencing public opinion. A poll commissioned by a Roman Catholic broadcasting station showed 76 percent of the respondents favoring limited legalized mercy killing.[21] Widespread acceptance of euthanasia has an inevitable impact upon the health professions as well, and the careful limits espoused by pro-euthanasia groups appear to be overlooked. In 1987, three nurses at Free University Hospital in Amsterdam were charged with giving lethal injections to three comatose patients. Apparently they had not consulted the patients' families or physicians, and they went on trial for murder.[22]

An Alarmed Opposition

The three professors mentioned earlier are in a distinct minority. They write, "Why do so many people favor euthanasia? They think that suffering is unworthy of man and too hard to endure. At this point, death is preferred to prolonging life. For many this type of reasoning has a deeper basis—that man must be free to control his own life and death." They conclude, "On grounds of our Christian faith, we reject the right of self-determination on this matter. We honor God's control over our lives even though it may seem that doctors have life in their hands."

The most well-organized opposition in the Netherlands comes from the Roman Catholic church. After guidelines restricting euthanasia were recommended by a government-appointed commission in 1985, a pastoral letter from Holland's Catholic bishops addressed the issue of "Suffering and Dying of the Sick." It is a comprehensive analysis of proper care for the sick, the reality of suffering, and theological reasons suicide and euthanasia are unacceptable options.

Significantly, it refutes the guiding secular philosophy that equates good health with the "value" of a person's life. The bishops write, "bodily deterioration alone does not have to be unworthy of man. History shows how many people, beaten, tortured and broken in body, sometimes even grew in personality in spite of it." They emphasize the needs for companionship, understanding, and reassurance that terminally ill people experience, and they believe "everything should be done to make it possible for the seriously ill and dying to stay in the circle of their own family or relatives."

The bishops also counter the idea of diminished "quality of life" by turning the tables on some advocates of mercy killing. "Dying becomes unworthy of man," they write, "if family and friends begin to look upon the dying person as a burden, withdraw themselves from him, [leave him] alone and lonesome." What determines our worthiness, in other words, is how we respond to illness and death (our own or another's), not what physical state we find ourselves in. The Catholic spokesmen are convinced that requests for euthanasia would become far less frequent if people knew more about suffering and death and were committed to providing appropriate kinds of care.

There is no suggestion, however, that dying should be prolonged. The patient has the right to determine what treatments he will receive, and the doctor has a responsibility to discern when death is near. At that point, the bishops say, "one should restrict oneself to relieving suffering by fighting pain, and by good and cordial human contact. One should abandon forms of treatment that prolong dying."

Again in contrast to some advocates of euthanasia, who avoid clear definitions or so broadly define their position that it encompasses all sorts of behaviors, the bishops clarify their terms. Euthanasia, they say, "indicates a deliberate intervention in the life of a dying person, someone who is mortally ill or seriously handicapped, with the intention to put an end to his life and suffering." Allowing a patient to die, or "passive euthanasia," is a concept often used to promote the idea of deliberate killing because it is practiced routinely in health-care settings. The bishops point out, "We see no reason to call this euthanasia. Such a person after all dies of his own illness. His death is neither intended nor caused, only nothing is done any more to postpone it."

The pastoral letter considers in depth the unique view of life contained in the Bible. Its application in the lives of believers and for the good of society is spelled out in detail. The bishops observe,

> Christians believe that human life proceeds from the hand of God. We receive it from our parents. But it is not the parents who create life.
>
> Whenever we give thanks for our life, but also when we protest and complain, we express how deeply we are connected to a personal God. . . . No man must ever unilaterally break up this fundamental connection of every man with the living God, by taking his life or having it terminated, not even when he is dying. . . . [B]elievers feel they owe it to him to accept their life with all its aspects, in joy and sadness, in its growth and decay, till the end.

One influential figure in the Netherlands who bridges the Roman Catholic and medical communities is Dr. J. A. J. Stevens, a physician and head of the Dutch Catholic Physician's Association. In a speech before a congress of the International Federation of Catholic Physician's Associations, Dr. Stevens told his colleagues, "among the reasons for euthanasia, the vast majority have to do with social circumstances, not with mere medical motives. . . . Experience shows that the terminal patient nearly always consents to the decision not to practice euthanasia if we tell him in a sensitive manner and promise him sincerely that his suffering will not be needlessly prolonged and will be alleviated as much as possible."

In response to the increasing incidence of euthanasia in Holland, Stevens says Catholic doctors there are making three commitments: "To pay more attention to our patients, to procure the best assistance and guidance [for the terminally ill], and to teach our students and young doctors [the art of] terminal care."

Conclusion

There is clearly a marked contrast in world view between the Dutch bishops and their counterparts in the pro-euthanasia movement. The debate, as well as the practice of active euthanasia, has progressed much further in the Netherlands than it has in the United States. Opponents of the practice find they are up against a well-organized cadre of apologists for the termination of life in a society where three-quarters of the population believe that assisted suicide should be legal. The bishops, as well as Protestants who oppose euthanasia, are in a pitched battle over what is best for Dutch society and for individual rights. Against the pressures of modern medical technology, aging, and soaring costs, they have a rough battle ahead.

In the United States, similar threads of social reality are weaving their way into our discussions of health care, public sentiment, and even theological reasoning. It is time to be on guard against subtle, persuasive arguments using terms such as "mercy" and "compassion." Particularly for Christians, there is an ample heritage of respect for life throughout church history. This is explored in Part 2, and it forms the basis for our own response to pro-euthanasia arguments.

Father Smith, opposing the slide to euthanasia and infanticide in Walker Percy's novel, illustrates eloquently why the danger is so great. Describing at length his early years in Germany, Father Smith reminisces about a young friend, Helmut, who served with Hitler's SS troops. Helmut was totally devoted to the German cause; he was extraordinarily brilliant and handsome. Of course, he never mentioned killing Jews. He spoke instead about preserving the purity of the German people.

To Father Smith's own horror many years later, he recognized how compelling Helmut's words and bearing were. Had Father Smith been German and not American, he would have joined Helmut, he confesses to the psychiatrist. He returns to Germany later as a soldier, fighting against Hitler's troops. At a hospital outside Munich, Father Smith learns children were put to death with drugs or gas in a sunny room with a single, white-tiled table. "Only later was I horrified," the priest recalls.

"We've got it wrong about horror. It doesn't come naturally but takes some effort."[23]

Chapter 2, Notes

1. Walker Percy, *The Thanatos Syndrome* (New York: Farrar, Straus, Giroux, 1987), 127-28.

2. Joseph J. Piccione, "You Die Your Way . . ." in *National Right to Life News*, 26 September 1985, 12.

3. "Public Attitudes on the Legalization of Euthanasia" in *Euthanasia Review* 1 (Fall 1986):179.

4. Joseph J. Piccione, *Last Rights: Treatment and Care Issues in Medical Ethics*, Free Congress Research and Education Foundation, 1984, 45.

5. Joseph Fletcher, *Humanhood: Essays in Biomedical Ethics* (New York: Prometheus Books, 1979), 149.

6. Ibid.

7. Ibid.

8. Richard Doerflinger, "Euthanasia: Gaining Ground?" in *Respect Life* (Washington, D. C.: National Council of Catholic Bishops, 1986), 23.

9. Ibid.

10. Fletcher, *Humanhood*, 152.

11. *The New York Times*, 29 March 1984, sec. A.

12. Judith Wilson Ross and William J. Winslade, *Choosing Life or Death: A Guide for Patients, Families and Professionals* (New York: The Free Press, 1986), 12, 13.

13. C. Everett Koop, "Ethical and Surgical Considerations in the Care of the Newborn with Congenital Abnormalities," in *Infanticide and the Handicapped Newborn*, ed. Dennis Horan and Melinda Delahoyde (Provo, Utah: Brigham Young University Press, 1982), 89.

14. Alan L. Otten, "In the Netherlands, the Very Ill Have Option of Euthanasia," *The Wall Street Journal*, 21 August 1987, 1.

15. Matthijs B. H. Visser, "Dutch Euthanasia: 'A Reasonable View,'" *The Hastings Center Report*, February 1987, 3.

16. Teresa A. Takken, "California and the Netherlands: Variant Understandings of Mercy Killing," *Ethical Currents*, August 1987, 6.

17. J. Douma, E. Schumman, and W. H. Velema, "Euthanasia: The Great Decision," trans. McKendree Langley, *Christian Renewal*, 23 March 1987.

18. Jeane Tromp Meesters, "The Member's Aid Service of the Dutch Association for Voluntary Euthanasia," *The Euthanasia Review* (Fall 1986):153.

19. Ibid., 154.

20. Ibid., 157.

21. Roland de Ligny, *The Washington Times*, 6 April 1987, sec. D.

22. Ibid.

23. Percy, *Thanatos Syndrome*, 254.

Chapter 3

Euthanasia and the Law:
Legal Trends in Health Care and Human Rights

*T*he evolving public attitude toward euthanasia is reflected in the law, and law in turn influences our thinking. This should be expected. In a republic such as the United States, the people ultimately determine the law by controlling who writes and interprets it. Voters directly elect legislators, who enact statutes governing when the termination of life-sustaining medical treatment is lawful and when it is not. Judges, who are either elected or chosen by elected officials, then apply these statutes and principles of constitutional and common law to individual cases.

As our society rethinks basic norms and values pertaining to the termination of medical treatment, the law appears in a state of flux. Legislators and judges rely on public opinion and the expert advice of physicians and ethicists in writing and interpreting the law in this area. Until the people and the experts agree on a standard of ethical conduct, the law will reflect their uncertainty.

Despite uncertainty, however, legislatures and courts must continue to decide these matters as they arise, and the people will look to the resulting statutes and judicial decisions for guidance. While the law cannot ultimately determine morality, it inevitably determines the standard of practice followed by most people. Indeed, the law provides the clearest gauge of what is actually occurring in America at this time—and what could happen to anyone stricken by a serious or terminal illness. Therefore it merits close examination.

A Question of Murder

The law governing the termination of life-sustaining medical care and treatment begins with a clear but fine distinction that opens the way to confusion and controversy in many actual cases. That distinction pits an individual's traditional personal right to refuse medical treatment against society's equally traditional stance against suicide. Both of these legal principles are rooted deep in the English common law and have long been recognized by American courts. Recent medical advances that can radically prolong the dying process have brought these two principles into conflict, as is apparent from reviewing both principles.

An individual's right to refuse medical treatment arises from both common (or judge-made) law and the constitutional right to individual privacy. Seventy-five years ago, the great American jurist Benjamin Cardozo wrote, "Every human being of adult years and sound mind has a right to determine what shall be done to his own body; and a surgeon who performs an operation without his patient's consent commits an assault, for which he is liable." Based on this principle, Cardozo found two physicians acted illegally in proceeding with a medically necessary operation to remove a tumor from a patient who had consented only to an examination.[1]

The 1984 case of Bertha Harris illustrates a more recent application of this right. Harris, then seventy-three years old and suffering from diabetes and circulatory problems, entered the District of Columbia General Hospital to have her gangrenous left leg amputated. Two weeks after the operation, hospital physicians found that the gangrene had spread to her right leg and recommended that it also be removed. When she refused, the hospital sought a court order authorizing the operation, claiming she would die without the surgery.

After questioning Harris, the court found that she "understands the nature and consequences of the treatment choice being presented with respect to the amputation of her leg, and chooses not to have the amputation at this time, believing at this time that an amputation is not necessary." Based on this finding, the court concluded that "the patient has a right to decline treatment, and there is no basis at this time on which this Court may or should interfere with her exercise of that right." While Harris did not accept the diagnosis that death was inevitable without surgery, she clearly preferred to die rather than undergo another amputation.[2] Under American law, she had a right to make that choice.

Prior to 1976, when the famous case of Karen Ann Quinlan opened the door for legal actions by relatives seeking to end treatment for terminally ill patients, most lawsuits involving the right to refuse medical treatment arose due to the patient's religious beliefs—and many did not involve serious illnesses. Perhaps the most common claimants were members of the Jehovah's Witnesses sect, who oppose blood transfusions on religious grounds and have successfully used this legal right to block transfusions even to the point of death. These rulings often cautioned, however, that a competent adult's right to refuse medical treatment gives way when it endangers others. For example, courts have mandated treatment where a clearly curable patient would leave a dependent child or the treatment (such as a vaccination) contributed to community health. Such exceptions rarely apply in cases where the unwanted treatment simply prolongs a patient's life without much chance for recovery.

Balanced against this right to refuse treatment is *society's historic rejection of suicide and euthanasia*. In his authoritative eighteenth-century compilation of English common law, which was widely used in this country, Sir William Blackstone wrote, "The suicide is guilty of a double offense, one spiritual, in evading the prerogative of the Almighty, and rushing to his immediate presence uncalled for, and the other temporal, against the sovereign [or state], who has an interest in the preservation of all his subjects, the law has therefore ranked this among the highest crimes." The traditional English punishments for suicide aimed at discouraging the act by confiscating the suicide's estate and by mandating an ignominious burial.[3] While these types of punishment have long been rejected in America, some states continue to outlaw actual or attempted suicide (though rarely punishing the offense). All states maintain laws against assisting others to kill themselves and actively participating in the killing.

A 1983 California case arising from an attempted double suicide illustrates the interplay of these laws. After drinking a quart of beer and telling their friends what they intended to do, two sixteen-year-old boys named Jeff and Joe drove a car off a 350-foot cliff for no apparent reason. As the car went over the edge with Joe at the wheel, he said to Jeff, "I guess this is it. Take it easy." Jeff died in the crash, but Joe survived and was charged with both murder and assisting Jeff's suicide.

In examining these two charges, the California Supreme Court wrote, "The key to distinguishing between the crimes of murder and of assisting suicide is the active or passive role of the defendant in the suicide. If the defendant merely furnishes the means, he is guilty of aiding a suicide; if he actively participates in the death of the suicide victim, he is guilty of murder." Supplying poison taken by a suicide victim constitutes assisting suicide, according to the court, while administering poison to a victim, even at the victim's request, constitutes murder. The court viewed a true joint suicide (where both victims are to die simultaneously by the same act) as more akin to furnishing means of death than committing murder, and found Joe guilty only of assisting suicide.[4]

Euthanasia raises these same questions of murder, suicide, and assisting suicide. For example, in a widely publicized 1985 case, a seventy-six-year-old retired engineer named Roswell Gilbert was charged with murder for fatally shooting his seriously ill wife, Emily, who suffered from Alzheimer's disease.

Prior to the shooting, Emily had pleaded with her husband to "please, let me die"—but this did not excuse his act in the eyes of the law. He was found guilty of murder and sentenced to life in prison for fulfilling his wife's request. Often, however, the legal system turns a blind eye to such acts, such as when a New York court recently dismissed murder charges against Keurt Semel, who had attempted to suffocate his elderly wife after she had taken an overdose of pills to end her suffering from lung cancer. The judge claimed to be uncertain whether suffocation or the overdose caused the death. Yet if Semel's act had clearly caused the death, the court would have found him guilty.

Drawing the Line

The legal principle against committing or assisting suicide comes into potential conflict with a patient's right to refuse medical treatment whenever that treatment is necessary to preserve life. The persons acting to end treatment, including persons declining treatment for the patient and the health care providers carrying out that request, are potentially liable for murder or assisting suicide unless those actions are protected by the patient's right to refuse treatment.

In general terms, these two potentially conflicting legal principles are reconciled by barring anyone, including doctors and relatives, from assisting a person to commit suicide, such as by supplying or administering poison, but by allowing an extremely ill patient to refuse medical treatment necessary for survival. This distinction between illegal suicide (or active euthanasia) and legal refusal of treatment (often called passive euthanasia) is quite clear when it involves the difference between shooting an ailing spouse (as in the *Gilbert* case) and refusing a risky operation (as in the *Harris* case). It becomes more blurred, and therefore more controversial, when the medical treatment is nothing more than routine acts necessary for anyone to live, such as providing food and water. A pair of recent California cases shows how hard it can be to draw this line.

In 1982, two Los Angeles medical doctors, Neil Barber and Robert Nejdl, were charged with murder for removing the tubes providing food and water to a comatose patient. The patient, Clarence Herbert, had suffered a heart attack following a cancer operation. Herbert's physical condition stabilized with prompt treatment, but he had suffered severe brain damage that left him in a coma from which he was unlikely to recover. After consulting with Barber and Nejdl, Herbert's wife and children requested the removal of all life-sustaining machines. Accordingly, a respirator and other intrusive medical equipment were disconnected, but Herbert clung to life due to the continued operation of autonomic bodily functions (such as breathing and heart beat) controlled by his undamaged brain stem. Two days later, the doctors removed the intravenous tubes providing food and water, and Herbert died.

The prosecution charged the doctors with murder on the grounds that they had a duty to provide food and water to all patients, much like parents have a recognized legal duty to feed their children. Although extraordinary treatment and heroic life-support measures may be withdrawn or withheld upon proper request in certain situations, the prosecutor reasoned that food and water were ordinary care that must always be provided. If the intentional ending of food and water causes death, as it did here, it constituted murder.

While the trial court judge accepted the prosecutor's theory and authorized a trial, the appellate court did not and halted the case. "The prosecution would have us draw a distinction between the use of mechanical breathing devices such as respirators and mechanical feeding devices such as intravenous tubes. The distinction urged seems to be based more on the emotional symbolism of providing food and water to those incapable of providing for themselves rather than on any rational difference," the appellate court reasoned. "Medical procedures to provide nutrition and hydration are more similar to other medical procedures than to typical human ways of providing nutrition and hydration. Their benefits and burdens ought to be evaluated in the same manner as any other medical procedure."

According to the court, the *benefits* of a treatment focused on its potential enhancement of the patient's quality of life while the *burdens* of a treatment involved its probable painfulness. "Thus, even if a proposed course of treatment might be extremely painful or intrusive, it would still be proportionate treatment if the prognosis was for complete cure or significant improvement in the patient's condition. On the other hand, a treatment course which is only minimally painful or intrusive may nonetheless be considered disproportionate to the potential benefits if the prognosis is virtually hopeless for any significant improvement in condition."

Viewed by this standard, even intravenous feeding was disproportionate treatment given the unlikelihood of Herbert regaining consciousness. As such, it could be stopped by Herbert without constituting suicide. Since he was unable to do so and had left no advance instructions, his next-of-kin could make the request for him. Complying with that request did not represent murder, the court ruled, only a reasonable exercise of the right to refuse treatment. Quoting from a 1983 report of the President's Commission for the Study of Ethical Problems in Medicine, the court stressed the importance that quality of life plays in making such a request: "So long as a mere biological existence is not considered the only value, patients may want to take the nature of that additional life into account." The court apparently saw little quality in Herbert's continued life.[5]

While the *Herbert* case was close enough to split the California judicial system, the line between wrongful suicide and legitimately refusing such basic medical treatment as food and water appears even finer when patients directly make the decision for themselves, as in the 1986 California case involving Elizabeth Bouvia. Only twenty-seven years old at the time, Bouvia had suffered since birth with severe cerebral palsy and was quadriplegic. By 1986, her handicaps had progressed to the point where she was completely bedridden and able to move only a few fingers and her head. She was physically helpless and wholly unable to care for, feed, wash, or even turn herself. Suffering continual pain from crippling arthritis, Bouvia lay flat in bed and was expected to do so for the rest of her life. Despite her severe physical handicaps, Bouvia was intelligent and mentally competent. She earned a college degree. She was married, but her husband left her, and she had suffered a miscarriage. Bouvia lived with her parents until told they could no longer care for her, so she moved to a city hospital.

As early as 1983, Bouvia expressed a desire to die. Since she could not perform any act capable of killing herself, she resolved to starve herself to death by not eating. Fearful for her life, physicians inserted a life-saving feeding tube down her throat against her will. Bouvia then filed suit to have the tube removed. The trial court refused her request, ruling that Bouvia was illegally trying to commit suicide with the hospital's assistance. The appeals court reversed this ruling, declaring "a patient has the right to refuse any medical treatment or medical services, even when such treatment is labeled 'furnishing nourishment and hydration.'"

Since the court ruling, Bouvia has not yet invoked her right to end tube feeding; she continues to live with her hard-won freedom to die. But the question remains, which court was right? Concluding that she could live fifteen to twenty years with feeding, the trial court ruled that the preservation of Bouvia's life outweighed her right to choose. The appellate court, in contrast, gave primary importance to Bouvia's right to refuse treatment. "We do not believe it is the policy of this State that all and every life must be preserved against the will of the sufferer," the court wrote. "It is incongruous, if not monstrous, for medical practitioners to assert their right to preserve a life that someone else must live, or, more accurately endure, for 15 to 20 years."[6]

The *Bouvia* case is unusual because she could express her own choice at the time, making it a clear case of either exercising a personal right to refuse treatment or committing suicide. Normally patients receiving life-sustaining medical care are comatose, brain damaged, or otherwise unable to refuse care, like Clarence Herbert. Traditionally, any appropriate available treatment would be provided to such incompetent patients, and hastening death by intentionally withholding it would constitute murder.

Since the recent advent of medical procedures capable of sustaining life as never before, several controversial means have been created for legally ending such treatment on patients who are then unable to decide for themselves. Some of those means allow patients to leave directions in advance; others authorize others to make the decisions for the patients. In theory at least, these means may be used only for seriously ill patients with little chance of recovery (such as Herbert and Bouvia), where the right to refuse treatment supersedes the policy against suicide and passive euthanasia. As the preceding examples indicate, the line can be difficult to draw. But courts and health care providers are doing so with increasing frequency, and the consequences must be faced.

Directions for Dying

Perhaps the most revolutionary legal response to modern life-sustaining technology is a document commonly known as a *living will*. Using such a document, persons can direct in advance that certain medical treatments not be used if they become terminally ill and are then incapable of participating in treatment decisions. Living wills represent a novel development in the thousand-year-old Anglo-American legal system. They manifest a new fear, expressed by many Americans, of being kept alive in a pitiful condition on some dreadful (and perhaps painful) machine, all the while wasting family financial resources better spent on the living. This fear simply did not exist in the past, when medicine could do little to prolong life for the terminally ill. As new medical options developed recently, many people sought ways to assert control over their final medical treatment, which they saw as essential to dying with dignity. For some, living wills fulfilled this need to plan for death.

Because the concept of a living will (or advance medical directive) does not exist in our legal tradition, legislation is needed to insure that dying pursuant to such a directive is legally recognized as a natural death. Otherwise, persons carrying out the directive risk prosecution for murder or assisting suicide, and the death, if deemed a suicide, might not qualify for payment of life-insurance benefits.

In 1976, California became the first state to authorize living wills. Thirty-seven other states have now followed suit—most in the past five years—so that two-thirds of all Americans can now execute valid living wills. "As a result," U. S. Surgeon General C. Everett Koop and Americans United for Life Executive Director Edward R. Grant observe, "living wills can no longer be viewed as a temporary legislative experiment in the field of death and dying."[7] Indeed, the only states not authorizing living wills by statute are the northeast block of Massachusetts, Michigan, New Jersey, New York, Ohio, Pennsylvania, and Rhode Island plus Kentucky, Minnesota, Nebraska, North Dakota, and South Carolina. Even in some of these states, courts have given at least limited recognition to living wills.

Most Americans support the idea of a living will as applied to truly extraordinary medical treatment. Indeed, a poll conducted in 1986 in conjunction with ABC-TV's "Nightline" found 70 percent of the respondents strongly favored advance medical directives. Leading senior citizens groups committed to protecting the elderly, including the National Legislative Council of the twenty-six-million member American Association of Retired Persons, endorse living will legislation, as do many religious groups. Even some right-to-life advocates acknowledge the appeal of the concept. "The stated purpose of the living will appears unassailable at first glance," noted John M. Janaro of the Child and Family Protection Institute. "This seems to embody both the principle of self-determination and the right to refuse extraordinary or futile medical treatment."[8]

Many right-to-life advocates, however, oppose the living will statutes now in place in most states. Although these laws typically claim to repudiate euthanasia, Koop and Grant fear that "passage of the living wills will make further proposals for more direct forms of euthanasia more palatable." Beyond this, current statutes differ greatly in what medical treatment may be ended, and when that termination may occur. "By using vague or broadly defined terms, such legislation typically provides the physician with significant latitude to withdraw even ordinary and beneficial treatment and food and water, for patients in noncritical situations," warned General Counsel James Bopp, Jr., of the National Right to Life Committee. Janaro agreed, cautioning "the language of the legislation is sufficiently ambiguous that the law can be manipulated."[9]

Comparing individual living-will laws reveals wide differences in scope and coverage. Some statutes, such as Maine's Living Will Act, specify that terminable life-sustaining procedures do not include administering food and water, but most leave this key issue up to the physician. Statutes also vary greatly in defining the "terminal condition" when the living will takes effect, ranging from the narrow Maryland definition that death be imminent even with treatment to the broad Iowa requirement of death "within a relatively short time" without treatment. Generally, individuals may specify in their own living will that food and water never be discontinued, and may try to tighten the definition of terminal condition. (Chapter 8 examines more fully the available options.) Nevertheless, some ambiguity is inevitable. As Koop and Grant caution, "No one can even theoretically contemplate all of the factors that will be operating when he becomes terminally ill."[10]

In some situations, *durable powers of attorney* offer a more flexible means of influencing future medical treatment decisions than do living wills. A durable power of attorney allows persons to choose in advance who shall make decisions for them if they are unable to do so for themselves. These documents originally were designed for property transactions, such as allowing a spouse to sell a house if the owner becomes incapacitated. Increasingly, they are being used to make health care decisions as well, and this appears legal, at least where the document so provides. Statutes in every state authorize competent adults to grant durable powers of attorney to any other competent adult. Procedures for doing so, and the possible consequences, are discussed more fully in chapter 7.

Unlike a living will, a durable power of attorney permits a person to choose in advance a health care *decision-maker* rather than a *treatment decision*. This is more flexible than a living will because the chosen decision-maker can tailor treatment decisions to the actual illness. However, the final decision is left to another. "Thus," according to James Bopp, "durable power of attorney is very dangerous since there is no real limitation on the right of the third party to withdraw treatment or care when the patient is incapacitated."[11] While some limits can be placed in the terms of a durable power of attorney, the only real protection lies in choosing decision-makers with similar values and then communicating as fully as possible the factors to be considered in making any decisions. In many instances, this may be preferable to letting the law impose a decision-maker after the patient becomes incapacitated.

Court Trends

Living wills and durable powers of attorney only cover the relatively few patients who have actually signed such documents. The vast majority of terminally ill patients are left under the newly developing legal doctrine of *substituted judgment*. Under this doctrine, the law empowers close relatives or other suitable persons to make terminal treatment decisions for incompetent patients.

This doctrine first gained public notice in 1976 with the *Quinlan* case. Karen Quinlan's father had requested court authority to disconnect a respirator from his comatose twenty-one-year-old daughter, who was diagnosed as permanently unconscious and dependent on the respirator for her survival. Concluding that Quinlan would have a legal right to refuse treatment if she was competent, the New Jersey Supreme Court authorized her father (as next-of-kin) to render his "best judgment . . . as to whether she would exercise it in these conditions." If she would do so, then he could do it for her and "the ensuing death would not be homicide but rather expiration from existing natural causes."[12] Even after the respirator was removed at the father's direction, however, Quinlan defied the medical experts by surviving in a coma for nearly a decade.

Since *Quinlan*, several state legislatures have tackled the question of who may terminate treatment for an incompetent person if that person has not signed either a living will or a durable power of attorney. Nine states have dealt with the issue by including in their living-will statutes provisions authorizing relatives to make treatment decisions for incompetent, terminally ill patients. These provisions typically confer this authority on the patient's spouse, if there is one. Otherwise, the authority passes to a majority of the patient's adult children, then to the parents, and finally to the next nearest relative.[13] While decision-makers are to consider the patient's wishes, they enjoy great leeway in making their decision. Thus, for example, in the case of an incompetent, terminally ill widow with three adult children, life-sustaining treatment could be withdrawn on the request of two children even if the third one objected. This situation would be avoided, of course, by the patient's designating a decision-maker in advance by a durable power of attorney.

Most states have not resolved this issue by statute, however, leaving it instead to the courts to deal with on a case-by-case basis. In this respect, *Quinlan* was simply the first in a line of cases from around the country addressing the various issues involved in terminating treatment for an incompetent patient. Following the precedent set by *Quinlan*, and without a living will or durable power of attorney to the contrary, state courts routinely allow the next of kin or legal guardian to remove respirators and other intrusive medical treatment from patients diagnosed as terminally ill or irreversibly comatose. Legal uncertainty remains about many key points, such as withholding food and water, the effect of the patient's own treatment preferences, and how close the patient must be to death. Controversial recent judicial rulings involving Claire Conroy and Paul Brophy highlight these issues.

Claire Conroy was an eighty-four-year-old retired cosmetics-company employee who had lived alone until she was placed in a nursing home by her only relative, a nephew, in 1979. By 1983, she was confined to her bed in a semifetal position. She suffered from heart disease, hypertension, diabetes, eye infections, and bed sores. Her left leg was gangrenous. Conroy could not speak, properly swallow, or control her bowels. She received food and water through a relatively painless tube that extended from her nose down her throat to her stomach. Yet Conroy could move her upper body somewhat, and would scratch herself and pull on her bandages. She moaned when moved or fed. Despite her greatly diminished mental capacity, her eyes sometimes followed individuals in the room, and she smiled when her hair was combed or her body rubbed.

Based on a medical diagnosis that Conroy's physical and mental conditions would never improve, her nephew requested the end of tube feeding. Believing the resulting death would be painful, her doctor refused. "She's a human being," the doctor stated, "and I guess she has a right to live if possible." The nephew then sought court authorization for removal of the feeding tube. Conroy died before the final court ruling in 1985, but the court rendered a decision anyway to clarify the doctrine of substitute judgment as applied to incompetent but not comatose patients whose life expectancies are less than one year.

According to the ruling, where there is a clear indication that an incompetent patient would have refused treatment, including tube feeding, then a family member or guardian can make the same decision on the patient's behalf. Such clear indication could arise from a living will, a durable power of attorney, or (as in Conroy's case) from prior statements. Where there is only some evidence that the patient would refuse treatment, then the substitute-judgment doctrine applies only where "the burdens of the patient's continued life with the treatment outweigh the benefits of that life." If there is no indication of the patient's wish, then treatment should continue unless it is inhumanly painful. Treatment must never be withdrawn from a patient who previously expressed a clear wish that it continue.[14] The Conroy decision underscores the need for everyone to make a decision regarding further medical treatment. Not to decide may allow a substitute decision-maker to make the decision instead, including discontinuing food and water.

The *Conroy* decision has received mixed reviews from all sides of the euthanasia debate. The Society for the Right to Die hailed it "as one of the most far-reaching decisions ever to be rendered by a court in the 'right-to-die' area." It particularly applauded the decision for approving living wills as evidence of a patient's wishes in a state that does not statutorily authorize such documents and for recognizing that tube feeding can be terminated. At the same time, the Society felt the court placed too many restrictions on exercising the right to die, especially by limiting the ruling to patients with short life expectancies.[15]

Looking at the decision from quite a different perspective, right-to-life advocate Janaro attacked it for conditioning treatment on the quality of life and classifying tube feeding as terminable treatment rather than necessary care. Koop and Grant, in contrast, saw a silver lining to an otherwise dark decision. While concerned that it legalized passive euthanasia for the small category of dying patients who would refuse treatment, they praised the decision for creating "an elaborate set of restrictions to prevent euthanasia from being practiced upon other patients." They cautioned, however, that future courts might ignore "the carefully wrought safeguards" of *Conroy*.[16] Grant saw this fear realized a year later in the case of Paul Brophy.

Brophy was a forty-six-year-old Massachusetts firefighter when he underwent brain surgery in 1983. He never regained consciousness after the operation and remained in a coma unable to voluntarily control his muscles or respond to verbal statements. Medical experts considered Brophy's condition irreversible. Apart from severe brain damage, Brophy's health was good. He was not in danger of imminent death and could have lived for years. All of his automatic bodily functions (such as digestion, breathing, and blood circulation) operated normally without mechanical assistance. Because he could not chew or swallow, however, Brophy received food and water directly into his stomach through a painless tube that was easily operated by a nurse or family member.

After Brophy had remained in a coma for over a year, his wife requested that tube feeding end because Paul "had no quality of life remaining." Mrs. Brophy, a practicing Catholic who attended mass daily and belonged to a prayer group, made the decision after extensive church counseling. Paul's four adult children, seven brothers and sisters, and elderly mother supported the decision. Brophy's physicians and his religiously affiliated hospital refused the request on the basis that withdrawal of food and water constituted the willful taking of human life.[17]

The family then sought a court order to end tube feeding. After the trial court had refused, a bitterly divided Massachusetts Supreme Judicial Court granted the request in 1986. The hospital, however, was given the option of transferring Brophy to a different institution rather than participate in what it continued to view as an unethical act. Brophy was promptly moved and died eight days later.

Four justices of the court, a bare majority, held that since "ample evidence" indicated that Brophy would have refused treatment, his wife could do so for him. "Of course," the majority observed, "the law does not permit suicide." But refusing life-sustaining medical treatment, including tube feeding, would not constitute suicide in these circumstances. "When we balance the State's interest in prolonging a patient's life against the rights of the patient to reject such prolongation, we must recognize that the State's interest in life encompasses a broader interest than mere corporal existence," the majority reasoned. "In certain, thankfully rare, circumstances, the burden of maintaining the corporal existence degrades the very humanity it was meant to serve." Concluding that Brophy "himself would feel that efforts to sustain life demeaned or degraded his humanity," the majority ruled that he had a right to refuse such efforts, including tube feeding. "Clearly," the majority added, "to be maintained by such artificial means over an extended period is not only invasive but extraordinary."

Three justices dissented sharply. "Brophy is not terminally ill, and death is not imminent," Justice Lynch wrote. "If nutrition and hydration are terminated, it is not the illness which causes the death but the decision (and act in accordance therewith) that the illness makes life not worth living. There is no rational distinction between suicide by deprivation of hydration or nutrition in or out of a medical setting—both are suicide." Justice O'Conner added, "Whether the court is establishing an absolute legal right to commit suicide or a right that depends on judicial measurement of the quality of the life involved, neither principle is consistent with this nation's traditional and fitting reverence for human life." Justice Noland was even more blunt: "I can think of nothing more degrading to the human person than the balance which the court struck today in favor of death and against life. It is but another triumph for the forces of secular humanism."[18]

Edward Grant described the *Brophy* case as a clear example of euthanasia. It represented a realization of Grant's fears that courts would ignore the safeguards in the *Conroy* decision against extending passive euthanasia to patients who were not terminally ill. The New Jersey Supreme Court, which had crafted the *Conroy* decision, took a kindred step in 1987 by recognizing the right to end tube feeding for Nancy Jobes, a thirty-one-year-old woman in much the same physical condition as Paul Brophy.[19]

Judicial Crosscurrents

Although *Quinlan*, *Conroy*, *Brophy*, and *Jobes* represent the dominant trend at this time, not all recent legal developments favor requests to terminate treatment. In 1981, for example, New York's highest court refused a request, made by the patient's mother, to discontinue life-sustaining therapy for a mentally retarded cancer victim. Because the patient had been retarded for life, he could never have formulated a reasoned preference regarding medical treatment. As such, the court ruled, no one could speak for him.[20] The Oklahoma legislature took a further step in 1987 by unanimously enacting a statute presuming "that every incompetent patient has directed his health care provider to provide him with hydration and nutrition." For all practical purposes under this law, food and water could be refused for an incompetent patient only if that patient had stated such a preference while competent yet already afflicted with the terminal illness.[21] While these two legal precedents place some limits on third-party decisions to end treatment, the bizarre case of Jacqueline Cole ultimately may play a larger role in discouraging such decisions.

On 29 March 1986, Jacqueline Cole, the middle-aged wife of a Baltimore Presbyterian minister, suffered a massive stroke. Her daughter, who was with her when it happened, recalled, "She raised her arm at one point and said, 'Christina, I am having a stroke, I can use my arm but I can't feel it.' Then she said, 'I don't want to live as someone other than who [I] was.'" She collapsed following this, and entered a coma in which she survived on a respirator and tube feeding.

Forty-one days later, Cole's husband asked Judge John C. Byrnes to authorize disconnecting the respirator. "It should be done," he testified, "because I believe that she would not wish to continue to exist in this present state and given even the slightest chance of recovery, I do not believe that she would wish to live anything other than a full, rich, qualitative style of life such as she enjoyed." The primary physician then described Cole's condition as "virtually hopeless, chances of her having any reasonably significant neurologic recovery are probably somewhere within a one in a hundred thousand, one in a million." Even if such recovery occurred, the doctor added,

"I would strongly suspect that she would be paralyzed bilaterally, that she would have significant difficulty moving either arm or either leg, that she would continue to need to be cared for completely."

Yet after hearing these arguments, Judge Byrnes hesitated. More medical testimony regarding Cole's condition was needed, the judge indicated, and the legal standards for terminating treatment must be laid out. Finally, the judge added, "too brief a time has elapsed, this is May 9th and the stroke was March 29th." Cole's husband was told to come back later with better arguments.[22] He never returned.

Six days later, Cole's husband recalled on the Donahue television program, "I was at the room with a friend of ours, who essentially had come to see Jackie for the last time. . . . He called out her name, and she opened her eyes." Within six months, she had almost completely recovered, except for the use of her legs and some short-term memory loss. She even remembered moments during her coma. "It was like swimming to the surface and then there would be a few sentences. I remember my husband particularly, and then he would just sink back down again. That's what I remember."[23] Thanks to Judge Byrnes's hesitation, she had time to break the surface and swim free.

Conclusions

The legal status of euthanasia in the United States remains uncertain a decade after *Quinlan*. During that period, most state legislatures have legalized living wills, and many courts have allowed surrogate decision-makers to end medical treatment for the terminally ill. To an extent this represents a logical extension of a patient's traditional right to refuse treatment, at least where the decision clearly reflects the patient's wishes. Some call this passive euthanasia; if so, then this form of euthanasia is legally occurring in this country. The American legal system continues to draw a firm line against active euthanasia and assisted suicide, however, with no statute or judicial decision condoning such acts.

Gray areas in the law have emerged between these two general principles. Is it lawful to withhold food and water? May the next of kin end treatment where an incompetent patient's wishes are unclear? Should treatment ever be discontinued for nonterminally ill patients? Although recent judicial decisions tend to answer yes to such questions, these rulings mostly come from a few states, particularly California, Massachusetts, New Jersey, and New York. Courts in other states may rule differently. Given the uncertainty, the surest way for persons to control the treatment that they would receive if they became incompetent is to decide in advance or confer the power to decide on someone who would make the "right" decisions. Ways of doing so are examined further in chapters 7 and 8.

Chapter 3, Notes

1. *Schloendorff v. Society of New York Hospital*, 211 N.Y. 125, 105 N.E. 92, 93 (1914).

2. *In re Harris*, Misc. No. 126-84 (D.C. Super. Ct., 4 June 1984), slip at 2-3.

3. William Blackstone, *Commentaries on the Laws of England*, vol. 4., 189-90.

4. *In re Joseph G.*, 34 Cal.3d 429, 436, 194 Cal. Rptr 163, 667 P.2d 1176 (1983).

5. *Barber v. Superior Court*, 147 Cal.App.3d 1016, 194 Cal.Rptr 484, 490-91 (1983).

6. *Bouvia v. Superior Court (Glenchur)*, 179 Cal.App.3d 1127, 225 Cal.Rptr 297, 300, 304-5 (1986).

7. C. Everett Koop and Edward R. Grant, "The 'Small Beginnings' of Euthanasia: Examining the Erosion in Legal Prohibitions Against Mercy-Killing," *Notre Dame Journal of Law, Ethics & Public Policy* (1986), 2:599.

8. John M. Janaro, "Death and Dying: Trends in Law and Medical Ethics," *Journal of Family and Culture* (1986), 2:46.

9. Koop and Grant, "'Small Beginnings,'" 606; James Bopp, Jr., "The Patients' Rights Act: A Comprehensive Approach," *National Right to Life News*, 27 March 1986, 11; and Janaro, "Death and Dying," 46.

10. 22 *Me. Rev. Stat. Ann.* sec. 2921(4); *Md. Heath Gen. Code Ann.* sec. 5-601(G); *Iowa Code* sec. 144A.2(8); and Koop and Grant, "'Small Beginnings,'" 602.

11. Bopp, "Patients' Rights," 11.

12. *In re Quinlan*, 70 N.J. 10, 355 A.2d 647, 664, 670 (1976), *cert. denied sub nom. Garger v. New Jersey*, 429 U.S. 922 (1976).

13. *E.g.*, 44 *Fla. Rev. Stat. Ann.* sec. 765.07.

14. *In re Conroy*, 98 N.J. 321, 486 A.2d 1209, 1217, 1232 (1985).

15. Society for the Right to Die, *Right-to-Die Court Decisions* (1986), NJ-6, NJ-7.

16. Janaro, "Death and Dying," 40-45; and Koop and Grant, "'Small Beginnings,'" 622-29.

17. *Brophy v. New England Sinai Hospital*, No. 85E0009-61 (Mass. Trial Ct., Norfolk Div., 21 October 1985), slip at 1-38; *rev'd* 398 Mass. 417, 497 N.E.2d 626 (1986).

18. *Id.*, 497 N.E.2d at 635, 637, 640, 642-43, 646.

19. Edward Grant, "Euthanasia Threatens Retirement States: Death Legislation Slated for Arizona, California, Florida," *The AUL Newsletter* (Winter 1986), 2; and *In re Jobes*, 108 N.J. 394, 529 A.2d 434, 438 (1987).

20. *In re Storar*, 52 N.Y.2d 363, 420 N.E.2d 64, 438 N.Y.S.2d 266, *cert. denied* 454 U.S. 858 (1981).

21. 63 *Ok. Rev. Stat.* sec. 3083.1-.5.

22. *In re Cole*, No. 8611053/CE49265 (Md. Cir. Ct., Baltimore Co., 9 May 1986), transcript at 10, 20, 39, 42, and 49.

23. Harry Cole and Jacqueline Cole, in "Donahue" transcript no. 11206, Multimedia Entertainment, Inc., 1, 6.

PART 2

CONSIDERATIONS

The euthanasia debate is often framed as an absolute commitment to one principle or another: either the sanctity of life or the quality of life. Do we preserve a human being simply because he lives among us and God made him, no matter how handicapped, impaired, or ill he may be? Or do we consider how intelligent he is or how well he interacts with other people or if he is capable of performing the essential tasks of daily life? Should the decision be influenced by whether he says he wants to die?

Philosophers and theologians have debated these questions for thousands of years, but they are doing so with a greater sense of urgency now than at many times in the past. In an increasing number of actual cases, these questions are passing from abstract theoretical speculations to considerations influencing life-and-death decisions involving seriously ill patients. The medical, societal, and legal sources of these developments were explored in the first part of this book.

In Part 2 we turn to religious and ethical considerations raised by these questions. Chapter 4 begins this by exploring the views of leading ethicists, theologians, and others who affirm either the sanctity-of-life or the quality-of-life principle, or views that attempt to forge a middle ground between these two principles. The remainder of this part examines distinctively Christian perspectives on euthanasia throughout the ages. Chapter 5 takes us from the time of Christ through the last century, and Chapter 6 considers twentieth-century Christian views on euthanasia and the broader topic of suffering and the Christian.

Chapter 4

Who's Who in the Euthanasia Debate:
Exploring the Views of Leading Ethicists and Theologians

*I*n the language of philosophers, the two opposing views on euthanasia arise from *teleological* ethics and *deontological* ethics. Teleological views are also known as *consequentialism*, basing a moral decision on the consequences of a certain action. In other words, whether an act is right or wrong depends on what happens as a result—nothing is considered inherently good or evil.

In contrast, deontologists base moral decisions on firmly fixed principles or rules. Some deeds, in their view, are always right and others are always wrong, and no set of circumstances ever changes that. Between these two views, some ethicists advance a modified consequentialism that permits a variety of exceptions to the rules.

These theoretical formulations take on flesh and blood with real urgency in the euthanasia debate. For example, let's imagine an elderly man, Mr. Bates, who suffers a stroke and appears to go into a coma. He is rushed to a hospital, where physicians stabilize him. Mr. Bates requires a feeding tube to receive nourishment, and the doctors automatically put it in place. A month later, nothing has changed.

At this point, Mr. Bates's four sons meet. They ask their father's attending physician to remove the feeding tube. Five years ago, they remind the doctors, their father signed a living will stating that he prefers no heroic treatment or resuscitation efforts when death is approaching. The doctors disagree, stating strongly that it is far too early to give up hope of at least partial recovery. At a stalemate, the doctors and the patient's sons agree to take their case to the hospital's ethics committee.

On the committee is a priest dedicated to the sanctity of life, and by training a deontological ethicist. He believes the Bible clearly defines right actions for people who are subject to God's sovereignty. And he affirms Vatican teaching that says, "Nothing and no one can in any way permit the killing of an innocent human being, whether a fetus or an embryo, an infant or an adult, an old person, or one suffering from an incurable disease, or a person who is dying. Furthermore, no one is permitted to ask for this act of killing, either for himself or herself or for another person."

Also serving on the committee is a young college professor who is preoccupied with finding ways to contain soaring medical costs. The professor is pragmatic, agnostic, and schooled in situation ethics.

When the committee convenes to consider the matter of Mr. Bates, the priest points out that feeding tubes are used so often in the hospital that they can hardly be considered extraordinary or heroic. Removing the ordinary care of feeding and fluids from this patient, he argues, is inconsistent with hospital policy forbidding any health-care professional from assisting the death of a patient.

The professor furrows his brow and draws deeply on his pipe. "What is ordinary care in the case of a thirty-year-old traffic accident victim with a good chance of recovery," he says, "certainly could be considered extraordinary if it is merely prolonging the dying of an elderly person." The patient's living will must be honored, he insists, and the unanimous agreement among Mr. Bates's sons deserves serious consideration. The consequences of removing the tube, he explains, will benefit all parties: the crowded hospital regains a bed, the financial drain on the Bates family is eased, and Mr. Bates slips away painlessly, rather than linger or face vigorous resuscitation if his heart stops.

Issues such as this hypothetical one occur with growing frequency in hospitals across the country. Understanding the nature of the debate means knowing the ethical stands that have been taken through the years. The most profound questions concerning how we live in community, how we care for those around us, and how we will manage ourselves in old age come to light in the debate surrounding euthanasia. The positions of various thought leaders are explained in this chapter to show how answers are being framed.

Truth or Consequences: Advocates of the Right to Die
Some of the best-known proponents of death with dignity have been introduced in previous chapters. In this section, we will explore their underlying philosophies, goals, and activities. They share in common a basic worldview emphasizing the consequences of an action as the primary guide to whether that action is right or wrong. They would ask, therefore, whether a good "result" will come of a decision to assist a patient—actively or passively—to die. This approach is also known as situation ethics, a system of ethics developed by professor and Episcopal priest Joseph Fletcher. His theories have fueled the euthanasia debate and, as seen in chapter 2, have influenced public opinion.

Joseph Fletcher. Undergirding Fletcher's consequentialist school of thought is his redefinition of what it takes to be considered a *person*. Society's understanding of life and death "have to change to keep pace with the new realities," he writes.[1] For Fletcher, the most important indication of personhood is the ability to think and reason. Without healthy brain function, he asserts, "the person is nonexistent."[2] In this framework, a person in a persistent vegetative state, a severely brain-damaged individual, or someone in an advanced stage of Alzheimer's disease would, at some point, cease to be members of the human community. Once they have been expelled by Fletcherian criteria, the inference is clear: We have no obligation to keep them physically functioning. Out of compassion for their lost personhood, Fletcher teaches, we may end their life.

To arrive at this position, Fletcher departs from orthodox Christian belief, rejecting the idea of God as an active presence in the world he has made. Fletcher writes, "We must rid ourselves of that obsolete theodicy according to which God is not only the cause but also the builder of nature and its works, and not only the builder but even the manager."[3]

Setting God on the sidelines, Fletcher calls for man to play God by engineering the social order. He points to abortion and birth control as evidence that we can successfully manage life, and writes that similar management is "equally imperative in death control."[4] He calls for "quality control" in terminating life, just as he advocates abortion for fetuses who fall short of his criteria for personhood.

Society for the Right to Die. Fletcher's societal impact on this issue is perhaps best reflected in an institution, the Society for the Right to Die, based in New York. According to its own promotional literature, the Society "believes that the basic rights of self-determination and of privacy include the right to control decisions relating to one's own medical care." In addition, the group opposes medical procedures that prolong dying, "thereby causing unnecessary pain and suffering and loss of dignity." Because a patient may not be able to express his own wishes as he dies, the Society seeks legal protection for dying patients (primarily through recognizing living wills) and for physicians and others who may otherwise treat patients aggressively to avoid malpractice suits.

The Society convened a conference of ten noted physicians in 1983 to define "The Physician's Responsibility toward Hopelessly Ill Patients." The resulting article appeared in the *New England Journal of Medicine* in April 1984. Phrased in careful, moderate language, the article argues for doctors to recognize how their training and the ethos of modern medicine combine to compel them toward sustaining life at all costs. "Although they should not be forced to act against their moral codes, they should guard against being excessively influenced by unexamined inner conflicts, a tendency to equate a patient's death with professional failure, or unrealistic expectations."[5]

In addition, they point out, "As society tries to contain the soaring cost of health care, the physician is subject to insistent demands for restraint, which cannot be ignored."[6] Even the use of the term "hopelessly ill" in the conference's theme conveys negative connotations, implying that "giving up" is the noble response.

There is not much in the Society's publications that would excite controversy, but Fletcher's radical views of personhood shed light on his ultimate aims. Determining the consequences of a patient's death means making projections into an unknown future. Could a cure be discovered soon? Might the patient go into a long remission? The philosophical framework of those who promote euthanasia as a solution does not adequately consider the "what ifs?" that cause many doctors to shun their ideas.

The Society for the Right to Die is an outgrowth of the Euthanasia Society of America, founded in 1938 by two social reformers, Charles Francis Potter and Eleanor Dwight Jones. The group promoted legislation allowing physicians, out of humane compassion, to assist the terminally ill in dying. Their efforts failed. A few years later, World War II and its gruesome reports from Nazi concentration camps led to staunch public opposition to any discussion of euthanasia.

After a decade of dormancy, the group's directors observed growing public concern over life-support technologies that prolonged dying. Under the leadership of Donald W. McKinney, a Unitarian minister, the Euthanasia Society of America began promoting the right of the patient to refuse treatment. This marked the beginning of the "patients' rights" movement.

In 1967, the Euthanasia Educational Fund was established to educate the public about the issue. At about the same time, the Euthanasia Society of America became inactive. In 1972, the Fund changed its name to the Euthanasia Educational Council, and in 1978 it became Concern for Dying. The final name change reflects the organization's problems in becoming identified with an idea most Americans found repugnant.

In the seventies, the original organization was reconstituted as the Society for the Right to Die, and its purpose again was to pass legislation. Since 1980, the two organizations (Concern for Dying and the Society for the Right to Die) have existed as separate, independent groups based in New York City. The Society has helped thirty-seven states pass living-will legislation, while Concern for Dying emphasizes education.

The Hemlock Society. More direct advocacy for euthanasia comes from the Hemlock Society, best known for trying to make assisted suicide legal. They call it "auto-euthanasia," or "rational and planned self-deliverance." It is seen as a justifiable response to terminal illness "which is causing unbearable suffering" to the patient. It is promoted as an option, too, for people with a physical handicap that makes existence "intolerable."

Hemlock has issued ethical guidelines for people contemplating euthanasia. These include maturity on the part of the patient, a search for reasonable medical help when a grave illness is diagnosed, informing the doctor, preparing a will, not involving others in assisting the suicide, and leaving a note apologizing for any inconvenience or embarrassment to caregivers or loved ones.[7]

Hemlock is perhaps best known for its book *Let Me Die Before I Wake* by founder Derek Humphry. By mid-1986, it had sold more than seventy thousand copies. It instructs readers how to commit "rational suicide in cases of terminal illness." People considering such an act are advised to ask themselves questions such as, "What does the immediate future hold for me? How much pain and indignation can I endure? Do I have any obligation to consider the other members of my family or those who are caring for me? Is there likely to be a cure for my illness soon?" A second widely circulated book by Humphry and Hemlock associate Ann Wickett is *The Right to Die: Understanding Euthanasia* (1986).

Humphry pleads for widespread education and social acceptability for suicide. For many people, he writes, "Just knowing how to kill themselves is in itself of great comfort and often extends lives."[8] He cites a Hemlock member in his nineties who wanted to end his life. The elderly man bought Hemlock's published guide on committing suicide and arranged for a European friend to provide the necessary drug dosage. Then he changed his mind. Humphry theorizes, "With the control and choice in his grasp, he had negotiated new terms concerning his fate."[9] Humphry does not speculate here about the possibility that a death wish might be acted upon in some future case, either by the patient himself or someone else, before there is time to reconsider.

James Rachels. A different apologetic for euthanasia comes from James Rachels, professor of philosophy at the University of Alabama at Birmingham. Rather than weigh the value of a patient's biological life against other values, as Fletcher and Humphry do, Rachels proposes "a new understanding of the sanctity of life."[10] Rachels recognizes the need to respect society's rule against killing. However, he says, the rule may be broken in some circumstances.

Rachels draws an analogy with the rules that govern highway driving. A driver knows that the basic rules of the road, such as driving on the right, are there to protect lives and prevent chaos. However, faced with a split-second decision as a car careens toward him head-on, the driver might break the rules of the road and veer left in the interest of preserving life.

Similarly, a physician might need to break the rule against killing in order to preserve the point of the rule, which is to promote human well-being and compassionate care for others. Rachels argues, "In some cases, killing does not involve the destruction of a life. A person in an irreversible coma, or an infant with such defects that it will never mature, is not the subject of a life; so they fall outside the scope of the rule thus understood."[11]

Rachels refutes the idea that intentions make a difference, so he sees no moral difference between a physician who allows a patient to die and one who takes decisive action to end a life. He also dismisses traditional distinctions between extraordinary and ordinary care. These are two cornerstones of Roman Catholic teaching on medical ethics.

Rachels contends that discerning a physician's intention might be helpful in understanding his character, but it is irrelevant to the question of whether his action is right or wrong. He illustrates this with an example of a terminally ill infant. One doctor determines to stop treating the infant because further medication is futile. The appropriate course of care appears to consist of providing comfort and routine care. A second doctor agrees with the decision to stop treatment, but his reasoning is different: He bases his choice for nontreatment on his hope for the baby to die as quickly as possible and thus escape further suffering.

Because both actions and results are identical, Rachels claims, the rightness or wrongness has nothing to do with the motivation or thought process of the doctors. However, Rachels does not address the question of whether a mindset of hastening death, rather than providing appropriate care to a dying person, might lead to an easier acceptance of lethal injection or other direct action. If a physician decides death is the best alternative for his patient, it seems a short step to conclude that the patient would benefit from some assistance in getting there.

Similarly, he considers the distinction between ordinary and extraordinary care outmoded and irrelevant. The terms are too slippery, he suggests, to offer any real guidance. Insulin injections would certainly be considered ordinary treatment for a young man with diabetes, but an elderly man dying of cancer who becomes diabetic might consider them extraordinary. Terminology like ordinary and extraordinary, or assessing the "benefits or burdens" of treatment, are dismissed by Rachels because they are so subjective. He says the only valid criterion for judging the rightness of a treatment choice, or a choice to kill, is the individual "patient's welfare and best interests."[12]

Rachels advocates legalizing euthanasia by making "mercy killing" an acceptable defense against a charge of homicide. He would leave the rule against taking life intact, but provide physicians a ready-made legal loophole if they can prove their victim requested death and suffered from a painful terminal illness.[13]

Assessing the Consequentialists

The strict consequentialist school of thought poses real problems for anyone who takes God's sovereignty over life seriously. In the words of Catholic moral theologian Richard Gula, this philosophical stand is arbitrary, too risky, and "erodes the character of a helping community of trust and care."[14] The values and "plusses" of human existence are selectively chosen by Fletcher and Humphry and limited to worldly concepts such as happiness and well-being. There is no room for Christian concepts such as the value of suffering. (This idea will be examined more fully in chapters 5 and 6.) Another flaw in the situational approach to decisions about euthanasia is its long-term risk. While the consequences may appear to be beneficial all around in the short term, no consideration is made of the long-range societal results of widely acceptable assisted death. Gula argues, "Wider application to the most vulnerable members of the community, such as the elderly and mentally and physically handicapped, may result from the lowering of psychological and social barriers to killing."[15]

Finally, the "klutz" factor feared by Daniel Callahan presents more than passing concern if the practice of euthanasia ever becomes entrenched. Pouring our collective health-care and policy-making energies into debates over whose life to terminate and when robs us of the capacity to explore alternatives. It is bound to decrease our sensitivity to what a person is really requesting when he or she says death is desired.

A Centrist Position

Ethicists who are termed "mixed consequentialists" take a middle of the road position, saying there is more at stake, morally, than just the consequences of an action. Life is viewed as a "basic" but not an "absolute" good. The Roman Catholic community has debated and studied these issues to a far deeper extent than its Protestant counterparts, and leading Catholic thinkers represent various understandings of this intermediate position. The centrist view combines an appreciation of free choice with a respect for the role and purposes of God in the world today.

Daniel C. Maguire. This Marquette University moral theologian comes closest to the consequentialist end of the spectrum while remaining distinct on several points. He advocates searching for the "moral object," or the essence of an act, which is based on more than just the immediate consequences apparent to an outside observer. An evaluation of the act in question (such as mercy killing) follows, based on all the facets of meaning and analysis a person is able to generate.

In his book *Death by Choice*, Maguire argues that it can be moral and should be legal to directly terminate life in certain circumstances. He points out that the will of God in the case of a direly ill person is not manifested only through the breakdown of the body. It may also be discerned by human sensitivity and reasoning. The problems we have in society today with regard to difficult life and death decisions, Maguire suggests, is that we have underestimated our dominion over life and death.

To counteract this, he calls on Christians to be participants in divine providence, since we have both the prerogative and the responsibility to discover the "good" and to choose it. Unlike those who favor euthanasia when they see it producing "good" results, however, Maguire emphasizes, "There should be no passion for euthanasia. Indeed, we should work for the conditions which make it less and less indicated."[16]

For him, the principle against ending life should weigh heavily in the balance of individual decision making. But it should not always hold sway. Other values—personal dignity, avoiding excessive expense, and self-determination—lay equal claim, in some cases, to the basic principle that life should not be terminated.

Richard A. McCormick. One of Catholicism's best-known bioethicists and moral theologians is Father Richard A. McCormick, a professor at Notre Dame University. His position on euthanasia, in contrast to Daniel Maguire's, comes closest to endorsing a sanctity of life view. Yet he remains willing to balance the value of life against other values, drawing more cautious conclusions than Maguire but ones that differentiate him from the thoroughgoing sanctity-of-life-view.

The biggest departure McCormick makes from the positions of other consequentialists is his view of the difference between omission (letting go) and commission (taking direct action) at the end of life. The positions outlined so far in this chapter share in common the idea that once a patient is dying, it makes no difference whether the doctor simply stops treating him, thus hastening death, or gives the patient a lethal injection. It is morally indifferent, the other ethicists say.

McCormick disagrees, arguing that choosing not to treat will not necessarily produce the same "consequences" as a lethal injection. The two are not morally identical, he says, based on the very criteria the consequentialists cite. Added to this is the deeper moral dilemma of devaluing a person's life when death is clearly imminent. That is no excuse for an action that in all other circumstances is considered murder. In this, McCormick clearly places principle above results.

He rejects direct termination of life because it would do harm to society at large, a consideration that is essentially ignored in the consequentialist school where the individual patient's outcome is paramount. McCormick is uneasy about the effect of direct termination on doctor-patient relationships, on setting standards of usefulness or burdensomeness, and the potential harm done to attitudes of health-care providers.

In an essay about life-and-death decisions regarding handicapped infants, McCormick explains why issues such as these cannot be confined to concern about the individual alone:

These are not private matters. What life-saving treatment is provided or not to the incompetent and handicapped is a matter of the gravest public concern. At
stake, after all, is the life of a human being, and by
consistent extension, the lives of many human beings. . . . [These decisions] are value judgments
involving assumptions about the origin, destiny, and
meaning of life and death.[17]

Life, for McCormick, is a basic good that can only be
outweighed by other values if there is an overwhelming "proportionate reason" for doing so. This exception to the rule sets
McCormick apart from the theologians and ethicists we will
consider next. McCormick does allow for choices to be made
in light of other considerations. But he draws the most cautious
conclusion possible.

The middle position attempts to accommodate a basic
moral injunction against killing with the need to recognize and
evaluate other values that can come into conflict with preserving
life. The extent to which those other values may weigh against
the affirmation of continued life diminishes from the Maguire
end of the spectrum to the McCormick side. Still, in each of
these frameworks a niche is provided for the possibility that
some values, in some circumstances, could outweigh the need
to preserve life.

A third philosophical position on euthanasia rejects entirely the idea that any humanly defined value could ever be
measured against God's gift of life to man. These ethicists
consider the sanctity of life to be incomparably valuable, and
they consider it man's duty to act accordingly.

Euthanasia's Active Opponents

Sanctity of life is the guiding principle for ethicists,
theologians, and others who oppose euthanasia. Here, too,
there is a range of opinion, but it is based on a framework that
finds life immeasurably precious when it is weighed against
any other passing value. Official Roman Catholic doctrine,

Protestant ethicist Paul Ramsey, evangelical leaders C. Everett Koop and the late Francis Schaeffer, and the National Right to Life Committee, among others, share common ground on this issue.

The Vatican Declaration. Roman Catholic teaching on euthanasia is contained in a 1980 document from the Vatican, "Declaration on Euthanasia." It solidly invokes the sanctity of life and places the suffering of the sick and dying in a clear, Christian context. According to the declaration, euthanasia is "an action or an omission which of itself or by intention causes death, in order that all suffering may in this way be eliminated."

Relying on revealed principles and God's sovereignty, the statement condemns "mercy killing" as a matter of principle, no matter how excruciating the circumstances of an individual case. "Most people regard life as something sacred and hold that no one may dispose of it at will, but believers see in life something greater, namely a gift of God's love, which they are called upon to preserve and make fruitful," the statement says.

Because of this, the declaration outlines the following three foundational judgments: No one can make an attempt on the life of an innocent person; everyone has the duty to lead his or her life in accordance with God's plan; and intentionally causing one's own death is "equally as wrong as murder." Suicide, the Vatican states, "is to be considered as a rejection of God's sovereignty and loving plan."

The declaration departs sharply from the perspective offered by advocates of death with dignity. It points out that the cry of a gravely ill person may sound like pleading for death, when "in fact it is almost always a case of an anguished plea for help and love," including human warmth, spiritual comfort, and the steady presence of loved ones and care providers.

Building on a foundation of firm opposition to killing, the declaration acknowledges cases where "the use of therapeutic means can sometimes pose problems." In other words, when a person is approaching death, Catholic tradition has held that "extraordinary" means of treatment are not morally required.

That term has become increasingly imprecise, the declaration admits, and in its place it recommends considering whether a medical treatment is "proportionate" to the situation or "disproportionate."

This answers Rachel's complaint that what is ordinary treatment in one case (such as insulin shots) might be extraordinary in another. The criterion of proportionate means, on the other hand, takes account of the patient's condition. The declaration offers four guidelines:

- The patient may use experimental techniques if he chooses.
- It is acceptable for the patient to consent to having those means cease "where the results fall short of expectations."
- If a patient refuses treatment that carries a risk or burden, that is all right. It is not the same as suicide, but rather "an acceptance of the human condition."
- When death is imminent in spite of treatment, those treatments may be refused, "so long as the normal care due to the sick person in similar cases is not interrupted."

William E. May. In the United States, Roman Catholic opposition to euthanasia has been articulated by moral theologian William E. May at Catholic University of America in Washington, D. C. His position parallels the writing of two Catholic philosophers, Germain Grisez and Joseph M. Boyle, Jr., who wrote *Life and Death with Liberty and Justice* (1979). These three reject what they consider dualism in the positions of those who favor euthanasia. In arguing for the termination of life, Fletcher regards the physical life of the body as a vehicle for the expression of true personhood. Apart from personality and cognitive ability, in other words, the body is useless.

These Catholic thinkers disagree. They view the human person as an integrated whole, consisting of body, soul, and spirit. Grisez and Boyle write, "Life is not only a condition which is necessary if a person is to achieve higher values. It is an intrinsic aspect of human flourishing; it directly contributes to the full dignity of the human person."[18]

Because life is a basic good, these three say, it cannot be acted against. They absolutely oppose euthanasia, finding that a choice against life can never be made since it balances life against other "goods" in a way that is morally illegitimate. At the same time, omitting or withdrawing treatment may be permissible if the care giver's intention is to relieve suffering, not to cause death.

Paul Ramsey. A standard bearer among Protestant opponents of euthanasia is Paul Ramsey, emeritus professor of religion at Princeton University. Ramsey views life as a gift, and Christian ethics as a matter of loyalty within a covenant bond. To be "faithful," he says, is the fundamental moral requirement of all our relationships. His adherence to principles instead of consequences is consistently clear in his writings.

Choosing death as an end result, for whatever reason, is unacceptable, according to Ramsey, because by doing so we violate the standard to which we are called as image-bearers of God. It is essential that we never abandon the care of a person in need or actively hasten death, because doing so violates foundational principles. Withholding or withdrawing care, on the other hand, may be acceptable in certain narrowly prescribed cases because stepping out of the way may be in accord with maintaining a faithful relationship with the patient.

Ramsey, writing in the early seventies, advanced a theory of "(only) caring for the dying." By this Ramsey allows for a physician to assess when a patient is at the point where further attempts to resuscitate or aggressively treat would be utterly futile. The insistent questions presented by the hard cases of the terminally ill and permanently incapacitated cannot be silenced by principles alone, Ramsey acknowledges. They must be addressed carefully and in the context of the patient himself—not on the basis of peripheral concerns such as the scarcity of beds or other hospital resources.[19]

We need, he writes, "to discover the moral limits properly surrounding efforts to save life," including the obligation "of intervening against many a medical intervention that is possible today." Our culture has a tendency to define death always as a disaster, and that tendency sets us up for a dangerous tilt toward triage, or "lifeboat ethics" regarding dying patients. He observes, "If we do not deliberately set aside the worst cases as a matter of public or hospital policy, the terminal cases will increasingly be neglected, because, paradoxically, of other demands upon sparse medical resources in a society that knows no other ethics in regard to dying patients than always by every means to keep them 'alive.'"[20]

Ramsey isolates two qualifications to his principle against euthanasia. First, care for the dying may be abandoned when the patient is "irretrievably inaccessible to human care." At the point at which the patient is completely indifferent to whether he is being aggressively cared for, comforted only, or dispatched with a lethal injection, the moral difference between direct killing and indirect hastening of death dissolves. This is, however, not the same as "mercy killing," Ramsey says. In this case, the care-givers are not breaking faith with their covenantal duty in relationship to the patient, according to Ramsey. "It is no contradiction to withhold what is not capable of being given and received," he explains.[21]

Second, the rule against intervening to hasten death may be qualified when medical treatments themselves become burdensome and intrusive. The rule in this case might be stated, "Always keep officious treatments away from the dying in order to draw close to them in companying with them and caring for them; never, therefore, take positive action to usher them out of our presence or to hasten their departure from the human community, unless there is a kind of prolonged dying in which it is medically impossible to keep severe pain at bay."[22]

On this point, Ramsey departs from the deontological positions taken by the Vatican declaration and other traditional Roman Catholic moral theologians. He permits exceptions to a strict rule against taking the life of a patient only when the human duty to care and comfort is no longer meaningful. That determination, he says, is appropriate for physicians, not moralists, to make.

C. Everett Koop. Surgeon General of the United States under President Ronald Reagan, C. Everett Koop is among evangelicalism's best-known statesmen and right-to-life advocates. He approaches difficult questions of treatment versus nontreatment and "extraordinary" versus "ordinary" means from the perspective of a physician. Koop, who directed pediatric surgery at Children's Hospital of Philadelphia, became famous for his work with disabled children and his success in separating Siamese twins.

He brings a concrete, common-sense perspective to the debate, differentiating clearly between providing a patient "all the life to which he or she is entitled," and (wrongly) "prolonging the act of dying." He explains,

> Suppose your daughter, age two, had a neuroblastoma, the most common tumor of childhood. I operated on her, gave her radiation therapy, and for two years she received chemotherapy. She did so well initially that you doubted the diagnosis could be cancer. But now you are seeing her slip, and we have to come to a decision. We can't operate, she can't take any more radiation, and I suggest we stop the chemotherapy.

> Why? Because if we continue the chemotherapy, she'll live about three months. She will have severe pain we can control, but will be like a zombie and probably become blind and deaf. If we stop the chemotherapy, she will die in only six weeks, but will not have the pain or become blind and deaf. I think discontinuing treatment is good medicine for this patient, for her family, and for society.[23]

Koop is exceedingly cautious, however, about granting anyone other than the patient—and perhaps the patient's closest family members—the right to make such a decision. Koop staunchly opposes euthanasia and cautions against even the most apparently innocuous step down a slippery slope toward it. He has opposed living wills and the assignment of durable power of attorney, seeing these as vehicles used by pro-euthanasia forces to win public support and promote the idea of choosing to die.

Koop speaks specifically as well about the responsibility of Christians to prevent misguided enthusiasm for euthanasia from fueling public policy. "You have to arouse the familial obligation toward the elderly in families," he exhorts. "If the elderly are not going to be abandoned, we will have to look to extended families in many instances. Churches, civic groups, and communities can all work individually or together to provide resources for the elderly that will lift them out of those areas where decisions are likely to be made against them."[24]

The vigilance Koop promotes involves discerning where the debate is going, aligning with cobelligerents, and negotiating for life even in the midst of a slippery slope. He predicts, "Some descent will be necessary." The debate needs, first of all, to be framed properly. He sees it not in terms of quality versus sanctity of life or more technical questions of types of treatment. Rather, he poses the question, "How ought we to care for those who cannot in one way or in every way care for themselves?"

From this point of view, "quality of life" takes on an altogether different connotation. "The quality of life we talk so much about," he observes, "is nowhere as important as in the reflection these decisions make in the quality of our own lives."[25]

Conclusion

The ongoing debate over euthanasia feeds on each new court case and each new medical advance. What remains constant are the basic philosophical principles leading ethicists, physicians, and theologians bring to their positions. It may appear, with a flood of recent court decisions, books, and high-tech developments, that questions of treatment versus non-treatment are relatively brand new. They are not. The euthanasia debate has a long history behind it, and in that history the seeds of the current debate are evident. In the next chapter, euthanasia is explored in history up through 1900. In chapter 6, twentieth-century outlooks on euthanasia are detailed from the perspective of personal faith. What does it mean to be a Christian in the midst of conflicting views and conclusions about euthanasia? This question will be addressed throughout the rest of this section.

Chapter 4, Notes

1. Joseph Fletcher, *Humanhood: Essays in Biomedical Ethics* (New York: Prometheus Books, 1979), 151.

2. Ibid., 16.

3. Ibid., 152.

4. Ibid.

5. Sidney H. Wanzer, M. D., et. al., "The Physician's Responsibility toward Hopelessly Ill Patients," in *The Physician and the Hopelessly Ill Patient: Legal, Medical and Ethical Guidelines* (New York: Society for the Right to Die), 1985, 8.

6. Ibid., 9.

7. Derek Humphry, "The Case for Rational Suicide," *The Euthanasia Review* 1 (Fall 1986):173.

8. Ibid., 175.

9. Ibid.

10. James Rachels, *The End of Life: Euthanasia and Morality* (London: Oxford University Press, 1986), 27.

11. Ibid., 28.

12. Ibid., 105.

13. Ibid., 185.

14. Richard M. Gula, *What Are They Saying about Euthanasia?* (New York: Paulist Press, 1986), 69.

15. Ibid., 70.

16. Daniel C. Maguire, *"Death and the Moral Domain,"* St. Luke's *Journal of Theology* (June 1977):216.

17. Richard A. McCormick, *How Brave a New World: Dilemmas in Bioethics* (Washington, D. C.: Georgetown University Press, 1981), 357-58.

18. Germain Grisez and Joseph M. Boyle, *Life and Death with Liberty and Justice* (Notre Dame, Ind.: Notre Dame University Press, 1979), 379-80.

19. Paul Ramsey, *The Patient as a Person* (New Haven, Conn.: Yale University Press, 1970), 116.

20. Ibid., 118.

21. Ibid., 161.

22. Ibid., 162.

23. C. Everett Koop, quoted in Ed Larson and Beth Spring, "Life Defying Acts," *Christianity Today*, 6 March 1987, 18.

24. From unpublished speeches delivered by C. Everett Koop, U. S. Surgeon General, in 1985 and 1986.

25. Ibid.

Chapter 5

Traditional Christian Perspectives:
Views on Euthanasia from the Time of Christ through the Nineteenth Century

*E*uthanasia is both a challenging new and a haunting old ethical issue for the Christian community. Christians now confront the issue in their everyday lives as never before due to the unprecedented medical advances over the past half century. Even the most commonplace life-preserving treatments, such as penicillin, modern anesthetics, and most vaccines, first became widely available during the lifetimes of many living Americans. Most of the more radical drugs and technologies capable of prolonging life and forestalling death appeared during the present generation, with such medical breakthroughs continuing to multiply as never before.

These developments have contributed to doubling the average age of Americans and vastly expanding the number of individuals dependent on ongoing medical care for their daily survival. The cost, burden, and suffering of many such individuals, some of whom have little chance of recovery, pose the questions of what medical treatment should be provided and when individuals should be allowed to die. While these questions have puzzled theologians and philosophers for as long as people have faced death and dying, the lack of life-prolonging medical treatments made the answers somewhat less pressing in the past. Yet the historic approaches to these ethical questions provide the foundation for the current debate.

Apostolic and Early Church Tradition

Many ancient civilizations extensively practiced both active and passive euthanasia, especially for the sick, the infirm, defective newborns, and the elderly. Certain Greco-Roman philosophies idealized suicide as a noble form of death. Even murder was not universally condemned, and the sick were often left to die or care for themselves. Indeed, at the time of Christ, Roman society typically linked claims of human worth to an individual's social class, nationality, or personal virtue rather than to human life per se.

On many of these points, Christ broke sharply from the dominant classical tradition. Mosaic law had, of course, condemned all murder in no uncertain terms and taught that all people were created in God's image (Genesis 1:26; 9:6; Exodus 20:13). Jesus confirmed and expanded on this principle (Matthew 5:21-22). In telling the story of the Good Samaritan, for example, Jesus admonished his followers to act like the Samaritan who had bandaged and treated the wounds of a traveler without knowing the injured man's identity, wealth, or social standing (Luke 10:25-37). The gospels also recount Jesus healing dozens of men and women, including persons from the lowest social classes and physical conditions. In describing the Last Judgment, Jesus reveals what the King will say to the righteous:

> Come, you who are blessed by my Father; take your inheritance, the kingdom prepared for you since the creation of the world. For I was hungry and you gave me something to eat, I was thirsty and you gave me something to drink, . . . I was sick and you looked after me.

When the righteous question when they did so, the King replies, "I tell you the truth, whatever you did for one of the least of these brothers of mine, you did for me." The King then judges the unrighteous for their failure to do these acts for him, saying, "whatever you did not do for one of the least of these, you did not do for me" (Matthew 25:31-46). These concepts of universal compassion and caring for the sick and needy revolutionized Roman society.

In the first three centuries after Christ's death, Christians carried these teachings throughout the Roman Empire with remarkable effect. While established Greek and Roman religious and ethical systems generally had not valued efforts to help the sick and other needy persons, early Christianity (building on Judaic traditions) encouraged them. Henry Sigerist, the respected Johns Hopkins University historian of medicine, describes the transformation brought by Christianity:

> To the Greek of the 5th century B.C. and long thereafter health appeared as the highest good. . . . The sick man, the cripple and the weakling could expect consideration from society only so long as their condition was capable of improvement. The most practical course to take with a weakling was to destroy him, and this was done frequently enough. . . .
>
> It remained for Christianity to introduce the most revolutionary and decisive change in the attitude of society toward the sick. Christianity came into the world as the religion of healing, as the joyful Gospel of the Redeemer and of Redemption. It addressed itself to the disinherited, to the sick and afflicted and promised them healing, a restoration both spiritual and physical. Had not Christ himself performed cures? Disease is no disgrace, is not a punishment for the sin of the sufferer or of others, nor does it render the patient inferior. On the contrary, suffering means purification and becomes grace. Illness is suffering and suffering perfects the sufferer; it is a friend of the soul, develops spiritual capacities and directs the gaze toward the Infinite. Disease

> thus became a cross which the patient carries in the
> footsteps of his Master. . . . It became the duty of
> the Christian to attend the sick and poor of the
> community.[1]

This new attitude inspired the doctrines and activities of
Roman Christianity. Early church leaders, including Polycarp
(c.70-155/160), Justin Martyr (c.100-165), Tertullian (c.160/
70-c.215/20), and Jerome (c.345-c.419), admonished Christians to care for the sick. Throughout the later Roman era,
Christians were noted for their willingness to treat diseased
individuals, including scorned plague victims. Historians Darrel W. Amundsen and Gary B. Ferngren note, "It was Christian
concern for all persons, who bore God's image, particularly
for those in need, that led to the establishment of the first
hospitals in the fourth century."[2]

Christian belief that God created man in his own image
and that Jesus died to save all mankind inspired a radical new
appreciation of human worth and dignity within the early
church. This appeared not only in a caring concern for the
sick, but also in a denunciation of such established Roman
practices as abortion, infanticide, euthanasia, and suicide. "For
us, indeed, as homicide is forbidden, it is not lawful to destroy
what is conceived in the womb," Tertullian wrote in the second
century. In addition to widely practicing abortion, pre-Christian
Roman society commonly killed unwanted children or abandoned them to die by exposure. "After Christianity was
legalized in the fourth century, it gradually introduced major
changes in the moral climate of the Roman world," Amundsen
and Ferngren observe. "Under successive Christian emperors
(beginning with Constantine), legislation was issued that aimed
at protecting newborn infants from exposure. Even more influential than imperial legislation, however, were the decisions
of church councils that condemned abortion, infanticide, and
exposure."[3]

A succession of early church leaders from Justin Martyr
through Clement of Alexandria (c.155-c.220) to Augustine of

Hippo (354-430) took an equally strong stand against suicide. "It is significant that in Holy Scripture no passage can be found enjoining or permitting suicide either in order to hasten our entry into immortality or to void or avoid temporal evils," Augustine explained. "God's command, 'thou shall not kill,' is to be taken as forbidding self destruction." Augustine clearly intended this to cover euthanasia. For example, to refute the Greek view accepting suicide as a means to end "pains and afflictions of the body," Augustine quoted the biblical passage about waiting with patience for heaven (Romans 8:24-25), and asserted "we wait 'with patience,' precisely because we are surrounded by evils which patience must endure until we come to where . . . there will be no longer anything to endure."[4]

Augustine's rejection of euthanasic suicide reflected not only his religious respect for human life but also his peculiarly Christian view of suffering. Unlike many pagan philosophers, Augustine did not view suffering as an evil to be avoided at all costs. For Augustine, mortal life simply represented a stage toward eternal life and not an end in itself. He viewed the transitory goods and evils of this world as distributed somewhat at random among both the just and the unjust. In spite of this, "when good and bad men suffer alike, they are not, for that reason, indistinguishable," Augustine observed. "For in the same fire, gold gleams and straw smokes. . . . So too the tides of trouble will test, purify, and improve the good, but beat, crush, and wash away the wicked."[5] Illness and physical affliction simply constituted one cause of worldly suffering.

Augustine's view of suffering and illness was firmly grounded in Scripture. Jesus repeatedly warned his followers that they would suffer persecution, just as he had (Matthew 5:10-12; Mark 10:28-31; John 15:20). Several apostolic letters presented physical affliction as a means of testing or discipline leading to endurance and spiritual maturity (Romans 5:1-5; Hebrews 12:7-11; James 1:2-8; 5:10-11; and 1 Peter 4:12-13). Perhaps Paul stated this point most clearly when he wrote, "though our outer man is decaying, yet our inner man is being

renewed day by day. For momentary, light affliction is producing for us an eternal weight of glory far beyond all comparison"
(2 Corinthians 4:16-17, NASB). Earlier in the same letter,
Paul had written about the physical injury and hardship he
suffered in present-day Turkey: "We were under great pressure,
far beyond our ability to endure, so that we despaired even of
life. Indeed, in our hearts we felt the sentence of death. But
this happened that we might not rely on ourselves but on God,
who raises the dead" (2 Corinthians 1:8-9).

To be sure, the New Testament is filled with accounts of
divine healing, and Paul admonished Christians against seeking
physical affliction as a means to greater spirituality (Colossians
2:23). Yet God did not always provide miraculous cures or
immunity from pain and suffering for believers. For example,
Paul wrote to Timothy about leaving a sick disciple behind in
Miletus and to the Philippians about the serious illness of
Epaphroditus (2 Timothy 4:20; Philippians 2:25-30). Paul himself suffered "a thorn in the flesh," which many Bible scholars
believe was a chronic illness or disability. "Three times I
pleaded with the Lord to take it away from me," Paul wrote.
"But he said to me, 'My grace is sufficient for you, for my
power is made perfect in weakness.' Therefore I will boast all
the more gladly about my weaknesses, so that Christ's power
may rest on me" (2 Corinthians 12:8-9).

This approach toward physical affliction is instructive.
Paul prayed for healing. Indeed, earlier in the same letter he
expressed a desire to die and thereby exchange worldly pain
for eternal bliss (2 Corinthians 5:1-10). But when relief did
not come, Paul accepted his affliction as a means of increasing
his dependence on Christ. The rejection of euthanasia coupled
with the acceptance of physical suffering, apparent in the early
church from Paul through Augustine, continued among succeed-
ing generations of Christians.

Medieval and Roman Catholic Tradition

The Roman Empire crumbled shortly after Augustine's
death in 430, and Western Europe entered the Middle Ages.

During this period, which lasted nearly a thousand years, political unity disappeared as the region was splintered first among shifting semibarbaric tribes and later into a multitude of feudal domains. Political disunity levied an awful toll in human suffering. Wars ravaged the countryside and leveled cities. The economic and social system collapsed, curtailing programs for health care and sanitation, constricting the average diet, and facilitating the spread of disease. During the period from 541 through 767 alone, sixteen waves of the bubonic plague swept across the continent. Political disunity was gradually counterbalanced by religious unity, however, as the influence of the Roman Catholic church spread across Europe.

In the face of severe human misery, medieval Catholicism maintained a stance against euthanasia while developing a deep appreciation of suffering as a means of positive Christian discipline and testing. Often such discipline was viewed as an indication of God's favor rather than as punishment. This appeared throughout the writings of the eighth-century English monk known as the Venerable Bede.

Bede's classic accounts of English history contain numerous accounts of individual human illness, injury, and physical suffering. Some pious sufferers were miraculously healed, others died quickly, while still others languished in worsening agony for years—but all accepted their plight as a divinely willed vehicle of spiritual chastening. For example, Bede recounted that to increase "the virtue of patience," the devout Bishop Benedict endured a prolonged terminal illness in which "Benedict, during three years, gradually became so paralyzed that all his lower limbs were quite dead." Throughout this illness, according to Bede, the bishop sought "always to be occupied with the praises of God and with teaching the brethren." Similarly, Bede wrote as follows about the final illness of Hilda, the saintly abbess of Whitby:

> After she had presided over the monastery for many
> years, it pleased the blessed Author of our salvation
> to subject her holy soul to the trial of a long bodily

sickness so that, like the apostle, her strength be made perfect in weakness. She was attacked by a fever which tortured her with its burning heat, and for six years the sickness afflicted her continually; yet during all this time she never ceased to give thanks to her Maker and to instruct the flock committed to her charge both in public and private. Taught by her own experience she warned them all, when health of body was granted to them, to serve the Lord dutifully and, when in adversity or sickness, always to return thanks to the Lord faithfully. In the seventh year of her illness she began to suffer internal pain and her last day came.[6]

Agonizing fatal illnesses such as those suffered by Bishop Benedict and Hilda were common during the Middle Ages due to the lack of effective medications and painkillers. Nonetheless, the Church firmly rejected active euthanasia and condemned suicide as a mortal sin.

These positions persisted within Roman Catholic doctrine long after the Middle Ages and into the modern era. "We must accept the sickness that God wishes, in the place he wishes, among the Persons he wishes, and with the inconveniences he wishes," the influential seventeenth-century Catholic theologian Francis of Sales (1567-1622) concluded. Illness and suffering were viewed as a valuable means of sanctification and spiritual improvement throughout the postmedieval period. The prominent Roman Catholic historian Marvin R. O'Connell explained, "Clearly, pain and illness were part of the purging process—a kind of good work—through which believers had to pass before they could experience the blessed vision of peace. To suffer, therefore, was to embark upon 'the royal road of the holy cross,' and those who suffered most were deemed to be the holiest of all."[7]

The highly regarded Catholic mystic Brother Lawrence (c.1605-1691) reflected this attitude in his letter to a sick friend: "I do not pray that you may be delivered from your pains, but

I pray God earnestly that he would give you strength and patience to bear them as long as He pleases. . . . Seek from Him the strength to endure as much, and as long, as He shall judge to be necessary for you."[8]

While Roman Catholic teaching accepted the inevitability of human afflictions and acknowledged their potential spiritual purposes, the Church did not encourage its followers to seek suffering after the medieval era. Following repeated outbreaks of self-flagellation among Catholics during the Middle Ages, Pope Clement VI condemned such practices in 1349. Since that time, the Church has regularly opposed self-inflicted mutilation and suffering while admonishing followers to preserve their life and health to the maximum extent naturally possible. "In the pulpit and the confessional the parish priest explained wellness, considered as a good in itself, under the rubric of the commandment 'Thou shall not kill,'" O'Connell noted. "This was an imperative that applied first of all to oneself; direct suicide as well as any form of euthanasia were dismissed out of hand."[9]

Unlike in the Middle Ages, however, Roman Catholic teaching no longer reached all of Western Christendom. Beginning in the fifteenth century, the spirit of reformation divided the church into a variety of Christian denominations. Protestants gradually developed their own views on illness, suffering, and euthanasia.

Historic Protestant Tradition

Early Protestants knew suffering firsthand. Many were persecuted for their faith. Even more suffered in the political turmoil and widespread warfare spawned by the Reformation. Others succumbed to the plague and other diseases that ravaged Europe during this same period. Protestantism was nurtured in a crucible of physical suffering. Confronting this situation, early Protestant leaders generally accepted the inevitability of human affliction and recognized its potential spiritual benefit for both believers and nonbelievers. Accordingly, afflictions were to be endured for as long as they lasted.

"Because nothing else is so effective in taming the flesh as are our cross and the suffering we must bear," German reformer Martin Luther (1483-1546) wrote in his preface to the eighth chapter of Romans, "He comforts us in our suffering by assuring us of the support of the spirit, of love, and all created things."[10] In this and other advice about enduring physical illness, Luther wrote from intense personal experience. Throughout his remarkably active life, Luther was plagued with almost constant ill health, including heart problems, kidney and bladder stones, an ulcerated leg, severe constipation and hemorrhoids, agonizing headaches, and recurrent respiratory difficulties. He did not view such illnesses as divine punishment, but as a natural consequence of man's sinful state to be countered with both prayer and medication. He felt God's presence and power even in his sickness. Indeed, after recovering from an illness so serious that his basic life signs were undetectable, Luther penned the great hymn of faith "A Mighty Fortress Is Our God," where he expressed confidence in God's triumph over spiritual foes with the concluding words, "Though life be wrenched away, They cannot win the day, The Kingdom's ours forever!"

Based on his own intense experience, Luther developed a rich theology of health and illness. "Luther did not think suffering good in itself nor something to be sought for self-improvement, but when encountered it could be the locus of wellness," Lutheran historian Carter Lindberg explains. "As one scholar has observed, 'Luther found healing precisely in his sickness not in escaping from it.' The theology of the cross was Luther's expression of the good news that God chose to meet and redeem his creation in its own limitations." Afflictions could serve to increase an individual's recognition of his utter dependence on God, and therefore should be accepted when they came. While Luther did not believe that Christians should unduly cling to life, suicide was never condoned as a means to end afflictions. Luther bore his painful and sometimes incapacitating illnesses until his natural death, and they enriched his theology. "It is not by understanding, reading, or speculation that one becomes a theologian," Luther once observed, "but through living, dying, and being damned."[11]

French reformer John Calvin (1509-1564) did not suffer as much sickness as Luther, and his theological writings did not devote as much attention to illness and wellness. Yet Calvin also accepted disease as an agent sent by God to cleanse his people, and never approved suicide or euthanasia as an escape from affliction. "We commend to thee those whom thou art pleased to visit and chasten with any cross or tribulation," Calvin wrote in his prayer for the afflicted, "all persons oppressed with poverty, imprisonment, sickness, banishment, or any other distress of body or sorrow of mind: That it may please thee to show them thy fatherly kindness, chastening them for their profit."[12]

Sickness came into the world with sin, Calvin believed, but was used by God for spiritual healing. In his great theological work, *The Institutes of the Christian Religion*, Calvin explained that while God "wills to provide for the health of all, he yet leaves no one free and untouched, because he knows that all, to a man, are diseased." Man should endure divinely willed physical affliction for as long as it lasts, for, as Calvin noted, "a man truly submitted to God's yoke only when he yielded his hand and back to His rod."[13]

Calvin carried this theology into practice when ministering at the sickbeds of his followers. In several letters he described the protracted final illnesses of friends and family—diseases which were allowed to run their natural course until, as Calvin described it in one such letter, the sufferer "gave up his pious soul to Christ."[14]

During the following century, English Calvinists carried similar teachings to Great Britain and America under the Presbyterian, Reformed, and Congregationalist banners. Theologian John Owen (1616-1683), known as "the Calvin of England," counseled believers that "God may deliver you, first of all, by sending you an affliction to mortify your heart."[15] At the same time, the influential English Puritan pastor Richard Baxter (1615-1691) advised Christians to seek the best medical care for their illness, yet warned them to be prepared for incurable diseases and death. Baxter, who endured persistent ill health and described his own preaching as that of "a dying man to dying men," instructed the sick to teach the well.

Interpreting the commandment "Thou shall not kill" in the authoritative Westminster *Larger Catechism* of 1647, English Calvinists implicitly denounced suicide and euthanasia by directing believers "to preserve the life of ourselves and others, by . . . patient bearing of the hand of God." Calvinist clergyman and scholar Cotton Mather (1663-1728) conveyed much the same message to colonial Puritans in New England, where he wrote, "O thou afflicted, and under distemper, go to physicians in obedience to God, who has commanded the use of means. But place thy dependence on God alone."[16]

Early English and American Baptist theologians, some of whom were influenced by Calvinism, held similar views on illness. "Throughout their history there is a remarkable consistency in the way Baptists have viewed suffering," Baptist historian Timothy P. Weber finds. "On the one hand, it is a result of sin and a fearful reminder of the Fall; on the other hand, it is often used by God to bring about spiritual growth in the Christian." For example, during his wife's severe illness, colonial American Baptist leader Roger Williams (1603-1683) counseled her to adopt a "humble, a patient, and thankful submission to the afflicting and chastening hand of God."[17]

The current evangelical and fundamentalist movements began emerging within traditional Protestant denominations during the late 1800s. Many founders of these overlapping movements reaffirmed the traditional Christian views on illness and death. The influential Baptist evangelist Charles H. Spurgeon (1834-1892) offered perhaps the best example. Spurgeon was afflicted throughout his later life with severe and often incapacitating illnesses. Yet he carried on his ministry whenever possible and came to appreciate the spiritual value of his suffering despite his earnest desire to end the pain.

In 1879, over a decade before his death, Spurgeon described his plight as follows:

I have suffered many times from severe sickness and frightful mental depression, sinking almost to despair. Almost every year I have been laid aside for a season; for flesh and blood cannot bear the strain, at least such flesh and blood as mine. I believe the affliction was necessary to me and has answered salutary ends; but I would, if it were God's will, escape from such frequent illness: that must be according to His will and not mine.

Near the end of his life, Spurgeon reflected, "I venture to say that the greatest earthly blessing that God can give to any of us is health, with the exception of sickness. Sickness has frequently been of more use to the saints of God than health has." Spurgeon saw similar blessings from the suffering caused by the illness of a loved one, for he immediately added, "A sick wife . . . might teach us lessons nowhere else to be learned so well. Trials drive us to the realities of religion."[18] Beneficial spiritual chastening passes not only to sick persons, but also to those who suffer with them.

Other nineteenth-century evangelical leaders shared Spurgeon's theological perspective on illness, if not his personal experience with it. "God allows pain, sickness, and disease, not because He loves to vex man, but because He desires to benefit man's heart, and mind, and conscience, and soul, to all eternity," evangelical Anglican bishop J. C. Ryle (1816-1900) wrote. "I exhort all true Christians who read this paper to remember how much they may glorify God in the time of sickness, and to lie quieted in God's hand when they are ill."[19] Calvinist theologian A. A. Hodge (1823-1886) of Princeton Theological Seminary agreed that Christians should recognize and endure sickness as God's "fatherly chastisement—a proof of love for our good, not a mark of anger or displeasure for sin," and added the observation, "Some of the holiest saints have been the greatest sufferers and for the longest time."[20]

The comments about illness by Spurgeon, Ryle, Hodge, and other late-nineteenth-century evangelical and fundamentalist leaders were, at least in part, directed against the spread of faith healers and the expectation of physical blessing associated with the emerging Pentecostal tradition. None of these Protestant traditions, however, endorsed suicide or euthanasia. Indeed, opposition to such acts was so fundamental that it was typically assumed rather than stated. Roman Catholics, of course, maintained equal, if not greater, opposition on both counts.

Into the Twentieth Century

Christians carried into the current century a rich theological and ethical heritage both of recognizing the spiritual value of enduring human suffering and of opposing euthanasia. This heritage now confronts new challenges posed by the availability of medical treatments capable of unprecedentedly (and perhaps unnaturally) prolonging life coupled with old challenges stemming from renewed interest in avoiding protracted terminal illnesses by prematurely ending life. Current Christian theologians, ethicists, clergy, and laity must apply established Christian truths to radically new situations in determining when and how to utilize modern medical options.

Chapter 5, Notes
_____

1. Henry E. Sigerist, *Civilization and Disease* (College Park: McGrath Publishing Co., 1970), 69-70.

2. Darrel W. Amundsen and Gary B. Ferngren, "The Early Christian Tradition," in *Caring and Curing: Health and Medicine in the Western Religious Traditions*, ed. Ronald L. Numbers and Darrel W. Amundsen (New York: Macmillian Publishing Co., 1986), 49.

3. Ibid., 50.

4. Augustine, *City of God*, 1:20, 19:4.

5. Ibid., 1:8.

6. Bede, *Vita Beatorum Abbatum*, as quoted in Darrel W. Amundsen, "The Medieval Catholic Tradition," in *Caring and Curing*, 77; and Bede, *The Ecclesiastical History of the English People*, 4:23.

7. Marvin R. O'Connell, "The Roman Catholic Tradition Since 1545,"' in *Caring and Curing*, 121.

8. Brother Lawrence, *The Practice of the Presence of God* (Old Tappan, N.J.: Fleming H. Revell Co., 1985), 55.

9. O'Connell, "Roman Catholic Tradition," 124.

10. Martin Luther, *Martin Luther: Selections from His Writings,* ed. John Dillenberger (Garden City, N.Y.: Anchor Press, 1961), 31.

11. Carter Lindberg, "The Lutheran Tradition," in *Caring and Curing,* 176-80.

12. From John Calvin, "For Afflicted Persons," in Charles W. Baird, *Eutaxia, or the Presbytrian Liturgies* (New York: Dodd, 1855), 39.

13. John Calvin, *Institutes of the Christian Religion,* ed. John T. McNeill (Philadelphia: Westminster Press, 1960), 1:705- 6.

14. John Calvin, *Letters of John Calvin,* ed. Jules Bonnet (New York: Franklin, 1972), 334.

15. John Owen, *Sin and Temptation: The Challenge to Personal Godliness,* ed. James M. Houston (Portland, Ore.: Multnomah Press, 1983), 135.

16. James H. Smylie, "The Reformed Tradition," in *Caring and Curing,* 211-13.

17. Timothy P. Weber, "The Baptist Tradition," in *Caring and Curing,* 290-91.

18. C. H. Spurgeon, *Autobiography: The Full Harvest, 1860- 1892* (Edinburgh: Banner of Truth Trust, 1973), 2:410-14.

19. John Charles Ryle, *Practical Religion* (London: Hunt, 1883), 360, 370.

20. Archibald Alexander Hodge, *Popular Lecures on Theological Themes* (Philadelphia: Presbyterian Board of Publication, 1887), 109.

Chapter 6

Current Christian Perspectives:
Contemporary Views on Euthanasia and Suffering

*B*uilding on the traditions and doctrines handed down since first-century Christianity, contemporary theologians have addressed hard questions about suffering, death, and dying. There is no consensus on these issues, but there is a common—and growing—concern about deeper questions of social covenant and shared values. Ethicist Stanley Hauerwas, at the Duke University divinity school, asserts that when we reduce the debate over euthanasia to questions of how we should behave in the face of particular hard cases, we have already lost the battle.

The appropriate question, Hauerwas contends, is not "What should we do?" but rather, "What should we be?" In other words, the fact that euthanasia is even mentioned as a realistic option suggests that certain moral choices and compromises already have been made. Hauerwas writes, "Suicide and euthanasia are not just descriptions of individual acts, but notions that form intentionality to have one kind of character rather than another."[1]

Society answers the question, "What should we be?" with the retort of another question, "Whose life is it, anyway?" The individual is supreme, and supremely in charge of his own coming and going. This is the mindset that gave rise to the "patient's rights" movement promoting autonomy of choice through living wills and other means. At best, it sets God aside from everyday involvement in the lives of people; at worst it ignores or dismisses him altogether.

How would a Christian response to the question, "What should we be?" differ from the response of contemporary secularism? In this chapter, we will examine five topics that shed the light of modern Christian scholarship not only on difficult medical dilemmas, but also on the larger questions of how we live together in community. These topics include God's sovereignty and the gift of life, healing and God's will, Christian views of death, the value of suffering, and the claims of the community.

Sovereignty and the Gift of Life

For centuries, as we saw in the previous chapter, medical attention for the body and spiritual nurture for the soul were linked. In the last century, however, the two pursuits became increasingly separate and autonomous. Until recently, therefore, attempts to heal sickness typically were pursued in the context of God's sovereignty over all of life. Modern civilization has grown more complicated and specialized, however, and the overarching interest and activity of God in these matters no longer appears to hold much meaning for many highly trained healthcare professionals.

God's sovereignty, however, is not altered by any technical advance or innovation man can dream up. It is one of God's inherent characteristics, and it is reiterated throughout Scripture. Far from being sidelined by contemporary religious theorists, God's sovereignty remains a cornerstone of Catholic and Protestant opposition to euthanasia and abortion.

What does it mean to say God is sovereign? It means we acknowledge his power and dominion over everything he has created—all of life, all of nature, all the frontiers of deep space. He established the world as it is and placed us in it. Sovereignty means God not only set things in motion at the outset, but he continues to work out his will and divine purpose through human history. He "works out everything in conformity with the purpose of his will" (Ephesians 1:11).

God had the authority to provide a means of salvation through his Son, Jesus Christ, who along with the Father has "all authority in heaven and on earth" (Matthew 28:18). Believers have the comfort of knowing that "all things work together for good to those who love God" (Romans 8:28, marginal reading) because he is sovereign over circumstances, accidents, and apparent twists of fate.

God's sovereignty is reflected in the names by which he is known throughout the Old Testament. He is "God Most High" (Genesis 14:17-20), "God Almighty" (Exodus 6:2-3), and "Sovereign LORD" (Genesis 15:2). And the Bible says his sovereignty is everlasting: "his kingdom will never end" (Luke 1:33).

Believers who accept the Bible as their authoritative guide for faith and practice acknowledge God's sovereignty in every aspect of their lives. It affects not just what they do from day to day, but who they are. The pervasive idea of life as a gift from God stems directly from the doctrine of his sovereignty. We are not the owners of ourselves; our life is, in a sense, loaned to us for a time.

The combined ideas of God's sovereignty and the gift of life illuminate Christian understandings of euthanasia. Because God is all-powerful and because he has created life and called it "good," Christians believe in the sanctity of life. It is a different concept from secular notions of human dignity or value, because it is based completely on what God has done for us, not on any personal capacity or potential or actual accomplishment. Father Richard Gula explains, "the sanctity of life, or human dignity and value, is not intrinsic to human life as such, nor is it dependent on the evaluation of other human beings or on human achievement. Rather, the sanctity of human life . . . is ultimately conferred by God."[2]

In terms of making specific medical decisions, the principle of the sanctity of life remains vague and does not offer fixed answers. But it addresses the deeper underlying issues raised by Hauerwas about what sort of society we want to promote. Gula writes that the sanctity-of-life principle "points us in the direction of enhancing the well-being of human life, inclines us to form certain kinds of rules to protect human life, engenders an attitude which fosters a strong bias in favor of human life, and encourages us to act in ways consistent with this bias."[3]

If God is sovereign and has given us the gift of life, then two truths are apparent: first, life is not ours to bestow or take. We cannot, in other words, "play God." Second, our stewardship over life must be consistent with God's own intentions and purposes. The application, in the case of euthanasia, appears deceptively simple: We must never intervene to hasten our own or another's dying.

There is a corollary to the principle of sovereignty, however, which is known as human responsibility or "free will." God is sovereign over us, but he will not coerce us to respond appropriately to him or to our neighbor. These two realities exist in tension with one another, not in contradiction. They place on us the awesome duty of discovering God's will and acting accordingly—even if we do not understand why or perceive any reason for it. God in his greatness shares dominion with us and charges us with the responsibilities of being good stewards, taking care of his creation.

It is at this point that sharp differences arise about specific instances where stewardship is being exercised—in hospitals, nursing homes, intensive care units. Joseph Fletcher and Paul Ramsey, both Protestants, reach opposite conclusions about treatment and care. Interestingly, to arrive at their divergent opinions, both of them appeal to God's love and mercy. One major difference between them is their understanding of the extent of God's sovereignty and the limits of man's responsibility.

Curiously, much of the Christian opposition to euthanasia as well as abortion is framed in terms of protecting "the right to life." While this may be a useful political term, it does not really fit the reality of life as a gift from God. The term "right to life" puts us back in the same box of individualism that characterizes the "patient's rights" movement. It is used as well by the "right to die" proponents, suggesting that it is up to the individual to determine for himself when and how he will live and die.

Communicating to a confused world the immutable principle of God's sovereignty is a clear task for the church and individual Christians. From that foundation, increased clarity about precisely how we exercise free will and our shared dominion can be expected. And people in critical decision-making positions might begin to see the importance of basic shared values in shaping the sort of society that is consistent with the purposes of a personal God who cares about his creation.

Healing and God's Will

A second area of Christian doctrine that affects the debate on euthanasia involves healing and the will of God for people who are diseased, handicapped, or injured in an accident. God healed in Old and New Testament times, and Christians generally agree that his healing powers have not, and will never, diminish. There is considerable difference of opinion, though, about when and why he heals today. Many believers see no contradiction between praying for health and seeing a doctor.

The most prominent emphasis on healing in contemporary American church life is found in the Pentecostal movement, which began at the turn of the century. Grant Wacker, associate professor of religious studies at the University of North Carolina, notes, "only a small minority of Pentecostals have ever claimed a miraculous healing themselves, but virtually all would have insisted that God readily breaks into history to heal any believer whose faith is sufficient."[4]

Pentecostals base their belief in God's healing powers on a literal interpretation of Isaiah 53:4-5 and its application to Jesus in Matthew 8:16-17. "He took up our infirmities and carried our diseases" and "by his wounds we are healed," the verses state. This is interpreted to mean that Christians should seek and expect physical healing just as they seek and expect spiritual salvation. These signs were restored to the contemporary church, the early Pentecostals taught, in order to further the spread of the gospel and announce the Lord's return.

Pentecostals stress that God's sovereignty over illness is as complete as it is in every other area of life. Since God is able to heal, and believers may seek healing from him, illness that persists must be explained in two ways: either the sick person's life was not measuring up to the demands of God's kingdom, or the faith of the patient was shallow.

Many early proponents of modern faith healing stressed the need for believers to accept God's miraculous work in their lives even if they did not see any evidence of a healing. "Claiming" a healing became an accepted part of Pentecostal faithfulness. It is easy to see how totally incompatible this view of the world is with any perspective that would tolerate—let alone promote—euthanasia. A tradition of distrust toward doctors and advanced technology, the insistence on being "separate" from the world, and faith in God's ability to restore people to health has kept Pentecostals away from critical debates on issues of bioethical concern.

Bridging the gap between Pentecostal and evangelical views on healing are two important figures from the nineteenth century: A. B. Simpson, founder of the Christian and Missionary Alliance, and A. J. Gordon, who founded the institutions that became Gordon College and Gordon-Conwell Theological Seminary. Both men experienced personal healing and became advocates of the practice. Simpson, the more insistent of the two, wrote in 1877 that sickness as well as sin originated with Satan. Sickness was therefore contrary to God's will, and healing always could be claimed by the believer.

Today, Pentecostals are far more willing to visit doctors, use prescription medicines, and come to terms with chronic conditions than they were in the early part of this century. The basic belief remains, though it is tempered with realistic accommodation to the need for modern medicine together with faith. It is manifested in figures such as Oral Roberts with his huge medical facility, the City of Faith, in Tulsa, Oklahoma.

Mainstream evangelicals considered the healing miracles of Jesus as providing "merely a foretaste of a fully redeemed world that still awaited fulfillment."[5] Just as sin had not been abolished, sickness and death were realities of earthly life, too. A major point of departure between Pentecostals and evangelicals was the question of where sickness originates. Satan was seen as the author of illness in the Pentecostal community, while evangelicals believed that God ordained sickness, disease, and death.[6]

In sharp contrast to the Pentecostal view of the sufferer as inadequate, evangelicals have said there is "no necessary correlation between godliness and health and that sickness and pain had beneficial spiritual effects in God's economy."[7] The godly, as well as the wicked, suffer bodily affliction. The "health and wealth" gospel that proclaims wellness and prosperity as rewards for believers has no basis in orthodox understandings of our dependency on Christ rather than on self.

Christian Perspectives on Death

The Christian view of God's role in "calling me home" has set believers apart from nonbelievers in the western tradition perhaps more decisively than any other issue. The twentieth-century evangelical view of death has shifted somewhat from the eternal perspective most often stressed before 1900. As the turn of the century approached, sober reflection on death and the transience of life increasingly gave way to a view that emphasized Christ's imminent second coming. Premillennialism, a fundamentalist doctrine, held that believers in the last days would meet Christ without ever having to die.

Expectant longing for Christ's return has, in recent years, been supplemented with an evangelical attention to life here and now. Political engagement, concerns about strengthening the family, social involvement, and ongoing relationships capture interest and attention. As abortion, euthanasia, and infanticide have emerged as controversial issues, evangelicals now are more likely to approach them as socio-political concerns, not strictly as issues relating to faith and piety.

As a result, a variety of views on death have emerged. Clearly evangelicals continue to emphasize the importance of personal salvation and being right with God before death. Foundational belief in a real heaven and hell has compelled spiritual care for the dying that stresses resurrection of the body and rest for the soul. Death is seen as "the last enemy" that Christ will conquer. It was imposed by God on humankind as a result of Adam and Eve's fall and has no part in God's coming kingdom.

Based on this view, some evangelicals see death as an intruder, not as a friend. It is an unnatural outgrowth of sin, and it is to be resisted, not embraced. Presbyterian pastor Paul Fowler writes, in connection with abortion, "the themes of life and death run through Scripture as diametrically opposed goals. God is the creator of life; death is the forfeiting of the life God created."[8]

The Christian facing imminent death or a life-threatening situation, however, understands that Jesus himself met death on the cross with courage and confidence. Through his death and resurrection, he bore our sins and became our Savior; he also modeled a Christian approach to death. The apostle Paul reflected this when he wrote, "To live is Christ and to die is gain," as he faced persecution and the real possibility of death. There is a sense of "looking forward" to death, not in eager anticipation, but in realistic expectation of being present with Christ himself.

This concept has informed Roman Catholic thinking, and it is expressed cogently by Gula:

On the one hand, death is something to be resisted, since the creation story shows it to be the result of turning from God and toward sin. On the other hand, death is something to be acknowledged, since the story of redemption shows it to be the means through which God is victorious in Christ. This way of understanding death gives "moral bite" to the distinction by setting limits on care. It does not support expressions of care which include forcing a person to the end of life, nor does it support holding on desperately to life when the end finally comes.[9]

Death brought on by the deliberate action of another person is forcefully condemned in the sixth commandment: "You shall not murder" (Exodus 20). This commandment is sweeping in its simplicity. It is understood by Jesus to condemn attitudes or intentions as well as actions. Even careless or negligent taking of life, as well as calculated first-degree murder, comes under its prohibition.

Expressed positively, protection of life is mandated by the Bible and articulated in the words of Christ: "love your neighbor as yourself" (Matthew 19:18-19). In the debate over euthanasia, love is cited as the reason some people favor mercy killing. The critical difference lies in how God's sovereignty and unconditional love for all mankind are understood. Critics of euthanasia say the chief motivating factor for active euthanasia often is the suffering of the patient's spouse or family. So the driving force of "love" can be cruelly misdirected. And death, God's final prerogative over earthly lives, can wind up being stage managed to suit the desires of people other than the patient.

Ethicist Hauerwas captures the tension between the Christian's grateful spirit toward life and his yielded spirit toward the reality of death. Life, he writes, "is a gift that is not a property to possess . . . but a task to live out. . . . [T]he whole point of learning to talk of life as a gift is to see ourselves as not our own possession nor anyone else's. Rather we owe our existence to others who sustain us and finally to the one without whom we could not be at all."[10]

The Value of Suffering

Another area where the church's voice departs radically from the world's is in its view of suffering. The letter from James exults, "Consider it pure joy, my brothers, whenever you face trials of many kinds" (1:2). Traditionally, Christians have perceived suffering not as a punishment for sin but as a positive—though unpleasant—way in which God works in our lives. One of the best current examples of this is Joni Eareckson Tada, injured as a young woman in a diving accident. Paralyzed from the neck down, Joni has developed tremendous reservoirs of compassion and encouragement for others who are physically limited. She has an effective ministry to those in similar circumstances, and she has expressed herself in painting and through speaking and writing.

This is not to say that suffering, in and of itself, is a good thing or something to be sought in a vain attempt to impress God or anyone else. Suffering, the book of Genesis reports, is an inescapable effect of the Fall (Genesis 3:16-19). Yet Christian thinkers affirm that the suffering that accompanies terminal illness and handicapping conditions has value.

Discerning God's purpose behind even the worst sort of suffering is at the root of Catholic theological views of life and death. When it cannot be discerned, as it often cannot, the response must then be one of faith alone. In its 1980 declaration on euthanasia, the Vatican wrote that suffering, especially at the end of life, "has a special place in God's saving plan; it is in fact a sharing in Christ's passion and a union with the redeeming sacrifice which he offered in obedience to the Father's will."

The Protestant view of suffering is different, but it shares in common with the Catholic view an appreciation for what God can accomplish through suffering in the life of the patient as well as in the care providers and family. Hauerwas's landmark work on the subject, *Suffering Presence*, details this eloquently and aims a sharp critique at modern medical philosophy. He writes, "The most decisive challenge which medicine raises for Christian convictions and morality involves the attempt to make suffering pointless and thus subject to elimination."[11]

And all too often, he points out, eliminating suffering means eliminating the sufferer, in the convoluted rationale of the mercy killing advocates. A view of life that aims to extinguish suffering is an incomplete and shallow one, Hauerwas writes. "To see the value of suffering we only have to ask what we would think of anyone who did not have the capacity to suffer (including God). Such a person could not bear grief or misfortune and thus would in effect give up the capacity to be human (or divine). For it is our capacity to feel grief and to identify with the misfortune of others which is the basis for our ability to recognize our fellow humanity."[12]

Ultimately, Christians who suffer discover in their trials an opportunity to draw closer to Christ and become more dependent on him. It is an instrument of spiritual maturity, if it can be received in that way or explained sensitively by others. Because God deals with each individual so personally and intimately, Hauerwas finds it repugnant when moralists attempt to define how much suffering is too much. "I do not think we can or should will a world without suffering, and the question is whether in allowing the suffering to die we are actually removing our own suffering."[13]

A Caring Community

Christians understand life, death, healing, and suffering differently from the world, and ideally they act differently when they approach these matters as well. The church, the body of Christ, is charged with being a caring community, its members committed first to God and then to the well-being and spiritual nurture of one another. When a believer is sick, handicapped, dying, or suffering in any way, the church has an obligation and an opportunity, in love, to embrace that person and keep him or her from feeling cast out.

Surprisingly, an Old Testament example of this occurs in the book of Job. Usually Job's "comforters" are cited in Christian teaching for their insensitivity, ignorance, and unhelpful comments, calling into question Job's faith and purity of life. But one critical fact tends to be overlooked: at least his three friends were present with him (Job 2:11-13). Hauerwas wryly observes, "they at least sat on the ground with him for seven days. Moreover they did not speak to him, 'for they saw that his suffering was very great.' That they did so is truly an act of magnanimity, for most of us are willing to be with sufferers . . . only if we can 'do something' to relieve their suffering or at least distract their attention."[14]

In the New Testament, perhaps the most striking instance of caring is Jesus' own willingness to touch the "untouchables" of his time—the lepers. In his healing hand was more than a physical cure. There was the warmth of a human welcome instead of the usual response of recoiling and withdrawing that greeted the afflicted people. In James 5, a pattern for caring and curing is spelled out that illustrates the distinctiveness of Christian community: "Is any one of you sick? He should call the elders of the church to pray over him and anoint him with oil in the name of the Lord" (5:14).

This is not merely a recipe for curing ills, but a commitment to be with the suffering person—at his beck and call, in fact. That commitment is the opposite of desertion and dehumanization, two sorry aspects of present-day attitudes toward the elderly and the infirm. Presence with the ill may be seen as obedience to God, as well as a model of the way in which he wants us to relate to one another. Hauerwas explains, "Thus medicine needs the church not to supply a foundation for its moral commitments, but rather as a resource of the habits and practices necessary to sustain the care of those in pain over the long haul."[15] If Christians fail to do this, consistently and without complaint, it will not be surprising that the world turns to mercy killing. It will know no other solution to seemingly intractable problems of an aging population and shrinking resources.

Skills of caring and ministry to the aged have emerged out of church communities since the first century, when the disciples debated how to take care of needy widows in their fellowship (Acts 6). Today this is evident in the hospice movement. In England, Cicely Saunders, a Christian woman, began the first modern hospice, St. Christopher's. Out of the hospice concept comes a commitment to spend time with the terminally ill without the trappings of advanced life-support techniques available in hospitals. Hospice offers the promise of a way to make euthanasia irrelevant. (The way hospice works is explored in detail in chapter 9.)

There is clearly an obligation for the community of the healthy to reach out and meet the needs of the infirm. But community implies as well a responsibility on the part of the person who is ill, handicapped, or severely distressed. The patients' part of the covenant of trust that characterizes a community is to do all within their power to remain alive. Trust is eroded when suicide is contemplated or when a patient goes a step further and requests assistance in committing suicide.

Our willingness or determination not to die, Hauerwas suggests, is "an affirmation that the trust that has sustained us in health is also the trust that sustains us in illness and distress; that our existence is a gift ultimately bounded by a hope that gives us a way to go on."[16] He affirms, "we must die in a way that provides for healthful and morally sound grief for those whom we leave behind."[17]

If not—if society succeeds in affirming a right to die or a right to commit suicide—"we must ask ourselves whether in accepting that right we have unwittingly affirmed a society that no longer wishes to provide the conditions for the miracle of trust and community."[18] Fears of old age, boredom, suffering, or "becoming a burden" are real and not groundless, but they need to be viewed in a completely different light—the light of compassion that does not dim even when the challenge seems overwhelming.

Chapter 6, Notes

1. Stanley Hauerwas, *Truthfulness and Tragedy* (Notre Dame, Ind.: University of Notre Dame Press, 1977), 102.

2. Richard M. Gula, *What Are They Saying about Euthanasia?* (New York: Paulist Press, 1986), 28.

3. Ibid., 31.

4. Grant Wacker, "The Pentecostal Tradition," in *Caring and Curing: Health and Medicine in the Western Religious Traditions*, ed. Ronald L. Numbers and Darrel W. Amundsen (New York: Macmillan Publishing Co., 1986), 516.

5. Gary B. Ferngren, "The Evangelical-Fundamentalist Tradition," in *Caring and Curing*, 496.

6. Ibid.

7. Ibid., 497.

8. Paul B. Fowler, *Abortion: Toward an Evangelical Consensus* (Portland, Ore.: Multnomah Press, 1987), 126.

9. Gula, *Euthanasia*, 44.

10. Hauerwas, *Truthfulness and Tragedy*, 108.

11. Hauerwas, *Suffering Presence* (Notre Dame, Ind.: University of Notre Dame Press, 1986), 24.

12. Ibid., 25.

13. Ibid., 34.

14. Ibid., 78.

15. Ibid., 81.

16. Hauerwas, *Truthfulness and Tragedy*, 111.

17. Ibid.

18. Ibid., 113.

PART 3

POSSIBLE RESPONSES

Accepting or rejecting life-sustaining medical treatment is a moral issue any one of us may have to face. Unlike decisions about the care of a handicapped newborn, which personally confront only a small percentage of people, choices about what to do in case of a coma or an incapacitating and possibly terminal illness may be required of any of us without warning.

The first part of this book examined the medical, societal, and legal developments underlying the increasing public debate over passive and active euthanasia. Prominent participants in that debate, and various past and present Christian perspectives on it, appeared in the second part. Based on this background, the final part of this book suggests possible responses to the issue for consideration by individuals, families, and churches. No single, simple response to the issue exists. There are altogether too many medical treatments and too great a variety of physical conditions to draw easy lines.

The following three chapters present different means for persons to take an active role in determining their final medical treatment, including the appointment of a surrogate decision-maker, preparing advance treatment directives, and considering hospices and other alternative forms of care. These alternatives should not be simplistically categorized as right or wrong. It is not *whether* you appoint a surrogate, sign a living will, or enter a hospice, but *how* that choice is made and implemented that matters. Further, no decision should ever be made without consulting spiritual, medical, and legal advisors. The final part of this book, therefore, is really a beginning—a starting point for personal decision making.

Chapter 7

Choosing a Surrogate:
The Court or You?

Rudolfo Torres, age fifty-seven, fell two stories at his Minneapolis home in mid-1983. While recovering in the hospital, he was strangled by a mis-attached restraining strap designed to keep patients from falling out of bed. Hospital personnel managed to resuscitate Torres, but not before he had suffered massive and apparently irreversible brain damage. Although not brain dead, Torres lapsed into a coma and was kept alive on a respirator.

The hospital did not know what to do with Torres. Clearly it bore potential responsibility for his condition and had assumed the burden of caring for him. Torres was obviously unable to request the termination of his treatment, and it was doubtful whether his only available relative, a cousin, could do so. Three months after the accident, the hospital asked the local probate court to appoint a conservator for Torres with full power "to petition the court for approval to discontinue treatment or withhold treatment, if deemed by the conservator to be in the conservatee's best interest." Acting on this request, the court named an independent third party as Torres's conservator and also appointed a lawyer to represent Torres in future legal actions.

The hospital then asked for a court hearing "on the medical care to be provided to Rudolfo Torres." At that hearing, held eight months after the accident, the conservator urged removal of the respirator. This recommendation was based partly on medical testimony that Torres had no chance of recovery as a conscious human being and partly on testimony by the cousin and a friend that Torres would want to die. Finding that ending life-sustaining treatment would be in the patient's "best interest," the court authorized the conservator to remove the respirator.

Torres's lawyer objected and appealed the ruling to the Minnesota Supreme Court. Since the patient did not feel any pain and had no dependents to support, the lawyer argued that "no conceivable interests of Mr. Torres could be served by his being deceased." The Supreme Court rejected this argument by speculating that "Mr. Torres may well have wished to avoid, as one writer vividly put it, 'the ultimate horror not of death but the possibility of being maintained in limbo, in a sterile room, by machines controlled by strangers.'" The lawyer countered that inadequate evidence existed of Torres's wishes on this point, but the Court disagreed, and sixteen months after the initial accident, authorized the conservator to remove the respirator. This authority was promptly exercised, and Torres died.[1]

Not to Decide Is to Decide
Torres's prolonged and costly legal proceedings, which represent just one of many such actions occurring across the country during the past decade, resulted in a court authorizing a stranger to end life-sustaining medical treatment for an incompetent patient. In passing, the *Torres* decision noted that "on the average about 10 life support systems are disconnected weekly in Minnesota" without court orders, following consultations between attending physicians and family members.[2] Because Minnesota has no living-will statute, these decisions typically occur without the patients' direct consent.

Presumably any decision to end life-sustaining treatment is based on some determination of the patient's best interest and reflect consideration of the patient's wishes. In most cases, however, the patient never chooses the ultimate decision-maker. Indeed, Rudolfo Torres did not even know the man who made the decision to end his life. Even when family members make the decision, they may not know the patient's wishes or share the patient's values. Decisions ending life-sustaining treatment for incompetent patients are being made daily in the United States. The only question is whether the patient chooses the decision-maker.

A decade or so ago, it might not have mattered much whether persons authorized others to make medical decisions for them. The law assumed patients would want to receive all available treatment necessary to prolong life. Accordingly, incompetent patients automatically received treatment. As discussed in chapter 3, this assumption has changed.

Beginning with the *Quinlan* decision in 1976, state courts regularly have authorized family members or court-appointed guardians to end life-sustaining treatment for incompetent patients. More recently, courts have included feeding and hydration tubes among the life-support systems that could be disconnected, even for some patients (such as Paul Brophy) who were not terminally ill. Legislatures in nine states have enacted laws specifically authorizing family members to end medical treatment for terminally ill patients in certain circumstances unless the patient has directed otherwise in writing.[3]

These changes underscore the need for everyone to plan ahead for treatment decisions. David N. O'Steen, Executive Director of the National Right to Life Committee, observed recently, "Resisting pro-death legislation alone and doing nothing else would provide protection only if there were a recognized and established presumption for treatment and care of incompetent patients. Since that presumption has been eroded, the absence of legislation simply leaves patients vulnerable to the wishes of the judiciary."[4] Although this comment appeared in a call for prolife legislative action, it logically applies to the need for personal decision making as well.

The surest way for individuals to control who will make treatment decisions for them in the event they become incompetent is to designate the decision-maker in advance. Otherwise a family member could easily assume that authority or a court could assign it to someone. Not to decide in advance leaves the door ajar for others to decide; it no longer prevents a decision to terminate medical treatment.

Durable Powers of Attorney

The standard legal method for persons to authorize others to act on their behalf is by granting a "power of attorney." Powers of attorney can be granted by any mentally competent adult to any other mentally competent adult. As used here, the term "attorney" simply means someone (technically called an "attorney-in-fact" or an "agent") empowered to act for another. This agent need not be a lawyer or an attorney-at-law.

Traditionally powers of attorney were used primarily in commercial transactions when the person granting the power (called the "principal") could not be present for some reason. In such situations the power automatically terminated when the principal died or became disabled or incompetent, on the grounds that the principal could not then act for himself, so no one could act for him. A principal also could revoke a power of attorney at any time. Obviously, traditional powers of attorney provide no basis to make health-care decisions for an incompetent patient.

Over the past two decades every state has enacted statutes authorizing "durable" powers of attorney. Typically these laws provide that a written power of attorney *remains effective* even after the principal becomes disabled or incompetent if the document states that the power shall not be affected by subsequent disability or incapacity of the principal. Most statutes also allow powers of attorney to *become effective* upon the disability or incapacity of the principal if the document so states.

Statutes authorizing durable powers of attorney originally were designed to make it easier for relatives to carry on property or other commercial transactions after one member of the family became disabled. But people quickly realized that durable powers also could be used for making health-care decisions, including terminating life-sustaining treatment for incompetent adults.

Because durable powers of attorney are entirely a creation of individual state statutes, both the method of creating them and the effect of doing so vary from state to state. Therefore a local lawyer should be consulted in preparing and using such a document. Widespread agreement exists, however, that a general durable power of attorney permits the designated agent to make health-care decisions within the limits contained in the document. Accordingly, durable powers of attorney are currently being used throughout the country to terminate treatment for incompetent patients without courts ever becoming involved.

An individual creating a durable power of attorney enjoys nearly complete control over the terms of the document. Although a standard durable power generally gives the agent total authority to make any lawful decisions for the principal, the document can limit the agent's power or discretion. For example, the document could provide that the agent may make decisions involving only real estate, in which case no health-care decisions could be made. Alternatively, the document could be limited to health-care decisions only.

To narrow the agent's authority still further, the document could allow the agent only to make decisions authorizing or continuing treatment, never to withhold or withdraw it. Even when broad authority over medical decisions is granted, the power to terminate tube feeding could be limited. In short, a durable power of attorney can be an extremely flexible document as long as the principal specifies in advance the limits he wants.

Perhaps the most important advantage of a durable power of attorney for making health-care decisions is that the principal chooses the decision-maker, thereby assuring, as much as possible, that the person chosen holds similar moral, ethical, and religious values regarding the sanctity of life. Beyond this, principals can explain their wishes regarding health care to their designated agents while they are still able to do so.

Choosing and advising one's own medical decision-maker provides significant added precautions that the principal's wishes will be respected. The multitude of possible illnesses and the ever-increasing number of treatment options make it impossible to include directions regarding all possible health-care decisions within the terms of a durable power of attorney. Today's terminal illness may be tomorrow's curable disease. Therefore to some extent principals must rely on the judgment and knowledge of their chosen agent to carry out their wishes. By choosing and advising agents carefully and by drafting the document as precisely as possible, durable powers of attorney give individuals a measure of control over what could happen to them in the event of a disabling illness or injury.

Asserting this control is not easy, however. Writing desired limits into the terms of a durable power of attorney inevitably requires soul-searching and often painful anticipation of disabling illnesses and dreaded treatments, culminating in hard decisions about life and death. Picking the right decision-maker and communicating treatment preferences also involves serious thought and difficult decisions, as does accepting the responsibility to serve as the agent for someone else. Yet all of this is necessary for durable powers of attorney to become constructive means of protecting personal values from surrogate decision makers picked by a court or imposed by statute.

In contrast, an unlimited durable power of attorney given without explanation to someone, even a close relative who does not necessarily hold similar values, can simply be a short cut for third parties to impose their wills. In such a situation, as James Bopp warns, "The only limitation on the third party's power to refuse medical treatment—which again, includes food and water—is that the durable power of attorney is to be exercised in the patient's 'best interest.' This is so broad and so vague as to constitute no real limitation."[5] With this warning in mind, the remainder of this chapter outlines terms and procedures individuals and their lawyers can consider in preparing durable powers of attorney.

Drafting a Durable Power

Complex considerations are involved in preparing a durable power of attorney for health care, but the actual terms of the document are simple. The power can broadly delegate authority over various personal and financial matters or narrowly limit authority to medical treatment decisions. In either case, the document should specifically state that health-care decisions are covered.[6]

State statutes differ on various details that should be included in a durable power of attorney, which underscores the importance of consulting a local lawyer to prepare the document. Despite these state variations, the basic terms of any durable power of attorney are standard and serve as the starting point for tailoring individual documents.

The sample Durable Power of Attorney for Heath Care reproduced here was prepared in 1986 for use by the leadership of the United States Senate Special Committee on Aging and for distribution by the American Association of Retired Persons in cooperation with the American Bar Association and the American College of Physicians.[7] It contains three basic parts that we will examine separately.

SAMPLE*

Durable Power of Attorney for Health Care

[Part 1]

I, _____ hereby appoint:

_____
name

_____
home address

_____
home telephone number

_____
work telephone number

as my agent to make health care decisions for me if and when I am unable to make my own health care decisions. This gives my agent the power to consent to giving, withholding, or stopping any health care, treatment, service, or diagnostic procedure. My agent also has the authority to talk with health care personnel, get information, and sign forms necessary to carry out those decisions.

If the person named as my agent is not available or is unable to act as my agent, then I appoint the following person(s) to serve in the order listed below:

1. _____

     name

     _____

     home address

     _____

     home telephone number

     _____

     work telephone number

2. _____

     name

     _____

     home address

     _____

     home telephone number

     _____

     work telephone number

---

*Check requirement of individual state statute.
 Source: Barbara Mishkin, Hogan and Hartson
 (except for notary blank).

[Part 2]

By this document I intend to create a power of attorney for health care which shall take effect upon my incapacity to make my own health care decisions and shall continue during that incapacity.

My agent shall make health care decisions as I direct below or as I make known to him or her in some other way.

(a) STATEMENT OF DESIRES CONCERNING LIFE-PROLONGING CARE, TREATMENT, SERVICES, AND PROCEDURES:

_____

_____

_____

_____

(b) SPECIAL PROVISIONS AND LIMITATIONS:

_____

_____

_____

_____

_____

_____

_____

[Part 3]

BY SIGNING HERE I INDICATE THAT I UNDERSTAND THE PURPOSE AND EFFECT OF THIS DOCUMENT.

I sign my name to this form on _____ .
(date)

My current home address: _____

_____

_____
(You sign here)

WITNESSES

I declare that the person who signed or acknowledged this document is personally known to me, that he/she signed or acknowledged this durable power of attorney in my presence, and that he/she appears to be of sound mind and under no duress, fraud, or undue influence. I am not the person appointed as agent by this document, nor am I the patient's health care provider, or an employee of the patient's health care provider.

First Witness

Signature: _____

Home Address: _____

Print Name: _____

Date: _____

Second Witness

Signature: _____

Home Address: _____

Print Name: _____

Date: _____

(AT LEAST ONE OF THE ABOVE WITNESSES MUST ALSO SIGN THE FOLLOWING DECLARATION.)

I further declare that I am not related to the patient by blood, marriage, or adoption, and, to the best of my knowledge, I am not entitled to any part of his/her estate under a will now existing or by operation of law.

Signature: _____

Signature: _____

Before me, the undersigned authority, on this _____ day of _____ 19_____, personally appeared _____, and _____, known to me to be the Declarant and the witnesses, respectively, whose names are signed to the foregoing instrument, and who in the presence of each other, did subscribe their names to the attached Durable Power of Attorney on this date, and that said Declarant at the time of execution of said Document was over the age of eighteen (18) years and of sound mind.

[SEAL]
My commission expires:

_____
Notary Public

Part 1: Basic Terms. The first part establishes the basic authority of the document. It simply calls for inserting the principal's name and the name, home address, and telephone number of the chosen agent. More than one agent may be named if the principal prefers to have co-agents, such as several family members, who must decide jointly. If more than two co-agents are named, the document should state whether decisions must be unanimous or may be made by majority vote.

The chosen agent usually is a close relative. However, it is also possible in every state except Florida (where the agent *must* be a relative) to pick a friend, church member, or pastor. It is unwise, however, to choose one's own doctor or health-care provider due to the possibility of conflicting interests. The central concern is to pick someone who will make decisions that reflect the principal's wishes and personal values.

The text following this preliminary information states the agent's authority to make health-care decisions and to obtain medical information on behalf of the principal when the principal is unable to make his own decisions. Space is then provided for listing alternative agents who would assume the power of attorney if the primary agent cannot serve. Listing alternative agents is especially important when the first choice is a spouse, because both husband and wife can be disabled in the same accident, leaving neither able to make decisions for the other. Even though alternative agents are less likely to serve than the primary one, they should still share the principal's values regarding the sanctity of life and know the principal's basic wishes regarding health-care decisions.

Part 2: Personalized Limitations. The second part presents the most difficult drafting issues in the document. It begins with the key phrase necessary to create a durable power of attorney—that the agent's authority shall continue while the principal is incapacitated. The sample also declares that the power does not take effect until the disability occurs.

Space is then provided in *subpart (a)* for a statement of *desires concerning life-prolonging care, treatment, services, and procedures.* This is the most important portion of the document for insuring that the principal's personal ethical, moral, and religious values are respected in any future health-care decisions. Although no specific language is required here, the standard document used in California presents four alternative statements for adoption.[8] These alternatives (which appear below) suggest a range of options—from requesting unlimited treatment to allowing subjective decisions based on the perceived quality of the patient's life. Other more detailed statements could be used just as well (and persons signing durable powers of attorney should include statements that accurately reflect their own wishes), but the following *four alternatives* present the basic issues for consideration.

> *Alternative 1*. I desire that my life be prolonged [and my death postponed] to the greatest extent possible, without regard to my condition, the chances I have for recovery or long term survival, or the cost of the procedures.

This alternative expresses the desire that every form of available medical treatment and care be provided to prolong life. The optional language in brackets, not found in the California statute, underscores the intention that death be postponed as long as possible even though the end of life is imminent. By expressing a desire for treatment, this statement counters the growing tendency of courts to authorize the termination of medical efforts based on the patient's presumed, but unexpressed, intentions.

> *Alternative 2*. If I am in a coma which my doctors have reasonably concluded is irreversible, I desire that life-sustaining or prolonging treatments or procedures *not* be used.

The second alternative requests the termination of life-support systems for irreversibly comatose patients, such as Rudolfo Torres or Karen Ann Quinlan. Of course, courts eventually authorized removing respirators from both of these patients without the benefit of a durable power of attorney, but only after long and expensive legal proceedings. If this is the only situation where termination is desired, then both alternatives 1 and 2 should be used, with 2 cast as an exception to 1.

> *Alternative 3*. If I have an incurable or terminal condition or illness [such that death is imminent with or without treatment] and no reasonable hope

of long-term recovery or survival, I desire that life-sustaining or prolonging treatments not be used.

Alternative 3 requests ending treatment for any incurable or terminal illness, rather than only a coma (Claire Conroy falls into this category). The optional bracketed language, not contained in the California sample, narrows this alternative to cover only cases where death is imminent even with treatment, which would exclude coma victims like Paul Brophy and other patients not near death. Here too, if this is the only situation where termination is desired, alternative 3 should be presented as an exception to alternative 1. Alternatives 2 and 3 can both be included in the document because they cover somewhat different situations.

> *Alternative 4.* I do not desire treatment to be provided and/or continued if the burdens of the treatment outweigh the expected benefits. My attorney-in-fact is to consider the relief of suffering, the preservation or restoration of functioning, and the quality as well as the extent of the possible extension of my life.

The final alternative gives the agent maximum legal authority to terminate life-sustaining medical treatment. It allows a purely subjective decision based on the principal's quality of life, much like the judicial balancing of burdens and benefits used to authorize Elizabeth Bouvia to refuse tube feeding. Exercising any greater discretion to end necessary treatment would cross the line into unlawfully assisting suicide or committing murder. As it is, many commentators would view this alternative as authorizing passive euthanasia. Persons using this alternative should not include any of the other options because they would be either unnecessary or inapplicable.

These alternative statements express general approaches to treatment but do not address *special provisions* or *limitations* applicable to every approach, such as the continuation of tube feeding. This is left to *subpart (b)*. The following three special provisions are offered for consideration, but others may be more appropriate depending on the principal's wishes and values.

> *Special Provision 1*. Notwithstanding any other authority provided by this document, my agent shall require in all instances that care, treatments, services, and procedures providing hydration and nutrition (including, but not limited to, nasogastric or gastrostomy tube use, intravenous feeding, subcutaneous or intramuscular hydration, parenteral feeding, or misting) be instituted and continued to a degree that is sufficient to sustain life.

The termination of artificially administered food and water is the single most controversial issue in the current euthanasia debate. As discussed in chapter 4, many Christian theologians utterly reject withholding food and water as always immoral while others accept it in certain situations. Courts across the country have displayed an increasing readiness to authorize these acts in recent years. Accordingly, under most standard durable powers of attorney, agents could direct the termination of artificial feeding and hydration unless a special provision or limitation to the contrary appears.

> *Special Provision 2*. Notwithstanding any other authority provided by this document, my agent shall never consent to any of the following on my behalf: abortion, sterilization, commitment to or placement in a mental health treatment facility, convulsive treatment, or psycho-surgery.

Durable powers of attorney for health care apply whenever the principal is legally unable to make personal decisions, not only during a terminal illness. This may occur at any time in the principal's life, such as following a serious accident or a mental breakdown. All medical treatments and procedures unacceptable to the principal should be specifically barred within the durable power of attorney so that an agent cannot authorize them. California law, for example, specifically prohibits an agent from authorizing certain reproductive or psychological treatments on the grounds that they are so controversial that one should only consent to them personally.[9] These procedures or treatments are listed in this second special provision. Individuals should consider adding other procedures or treatments to this list based on personal wishes and values.

> *Special Provision 3.* Notwithstanding any other authority provided by this document, my agent shall require in all instances that care, treatment, services, and procedures deemed necessary to provide comfort care or to alleviate pain shall be instituted and continued.

Many living-will statutes specifically exempt comfort care and the alleviation of pain from the life-sustaining medical treatments that may be withdrawn or withheld from a patient. Courts have done the same in the absence of a living will or durable power of attorney.[10] This special provision makes clear that the person granting a durable power of attorney also wants to receive all available health care necessary to provide comfort and to reduce pain. Other special provisions and limitations could be added, and these altered, to reflect individual intentions, but these three samples cover the issues of most widespread concern.

Part 3: Signed, Sealed, and Delivered. The final part of the sample document contains formal or technical items needed to make the document legally binding and enforceable. These items are prescribed by statute in every state. Although legal requirements for executing durable powers of attorney are similar throughout the country, subtle variations do exist. These variations are important because even minor deficiencies can invalidate the document.

The sample Durable Power of Attorney for Heath Care includes standard items common to most states. Those items should be included in every document, even if not required by the principal's current home state, in case the durable power must be used in another state. This could occur, for example, if the principal became ill while traveling and required medical attention out of state. Nevertheless, persons executing durable powers of attorney should always consult with a local lawyer to insure that all legal formalities required by the state of residence are satisfied.

All states require that a durable power of attorney be signed and dated by the principal. A current home address should also be provided, as shown in the sample document. Most states also require that two witnesses sign the document. A few states provide that at least one witness neither be related to the principal nor entitled to any part of the principal's estate. Additional requirements are imposed by some jurisdictions.

Steps remain even after executing a durable power of attorney. For starters, the principal should continue the process of discussing treatment preferences with designated agents and health-care providers. Wishes with respect to new medical treatments and emerging illnesses need to be thought through, communicated to agents, and perhaps incorporated into revised documents. Beyond this, copies of the durable power of attorney should be distributed to each primary and alternative agent, health-care providers, and close relatives. Finally, some state statutes provide that durable powers of attorney automatically expire after set terms (such as seven years in California), so that new documents must be drawn up periodically as advised by a local lawyer.[11] These precautions help assure that an individual's health-care intentions will be respected during any future period of disability.

Conclusions

Surrogate decision makers are ending life-sustaining medical treatment for incompetent patients in an ever-increasing number of cases throughout the United States. Some act with direct judicial authority. Others utilize statutory powers. Most simply act as next-of-kin upon consultation with the attending physician.

Although many cases involve ending truly extraordinary treatment for clearly terminal patients who undoubtedly would have made the same decision themselves, an apparently growing number of cases are less clear cut. For example, feeding tubes and other life-support systems have been removed from incompetent patients who have never clearly expressed such a desire, with the decision based on subjective considerations about the patient's quality of life.

Judicial opinions differ sharply on rulings of this type. Massachusetts Supreme Court Justice Joseph R. Noland saw "another triumph for the forces of secular humanism" in *Brophy*. In contrast, the Minnesota Supreme Court viewed *Torres* as a victory for human dignity over "the ultimate horror . . . of being maintained in limbo, in a sterile room, by machines controlled by strangers."[12]

Durable powers of attorney for health care offer a flexible method for individuals to reduce the danger that unwanted surrogate decision-makers could choose their medical treatment in a manner inconsistent with their wishes and values. When ruling on treatment for incompetent patients, courts customarily enforce any directions expressed by the patients before they became disabled. Further, courts rarely displace a person's own handpicked surrogate decision-maker.

Carefully drafted durable powers of attorney can provide both of these defenses against unwanted decisions imposed by a court or a relative. By doing so they offer one significant, albeit imperfect, means of planning for the future and maintaining personal values to life's end. Living wills, which represent a less flexible and more controversial means of accomplishing the same end, are discussed in the next chapter.

Chapter 7, Notes

1. *In re the Conservatorship of Torres*, 257 N.W.2d 332, 334-35, 340 (Minn. 1984).

2. *Id.*, 357 N.W.2d at 341.

3. *E.g., Fla. Stat.* sec. 765.07.

4. David N. O'Steen, "Climbing Up the Slippery Slope," in *Window on the Future: The Pro-Life Year in Review, 1986*, ed. Dave Andrusko (Washington, D. C.: National Right to Life Committee, 1987), 84.

5. James Bopp, Jr., "The Patients' Rights Act: A Comprehensive Approach," *National Right to Life News*, 27 March 1986, 11.

6. See, *Op. Att'y Gen.* No. 84-F16 (N.Y. 1984).

7. Barbara Mishkin, *A Matter of Choice: Planning Ahead for Health Care Decisions* (Washington, D. C.: American Association of Retired Persons, 1986), 43-44.

8. *Id.*, at 49.

9. *Cal. Civil Code* sec 2435 (West).

10. *E.g., Iowa Code* sec. 144A.2(5); and *Bouvia v. Superior Court (Glenchur)*, 179 Cal.App.3d 1127, 225 Cal. Rptr. 297, 306 (1986).

11. *Cal. Civil Code* sec. 2436.5.

12. *Brophy v. New England Sinai Hospital*, 398 Mass. 417, 497 N.E.2d 626, 640 (1986); and *In re Torres*, 357 N.W.2d at 340.

Chapter 8

Living Wills:
Solution or Surrender?

A ll across America, the courts and surrogate decision-makers are ending life-sustaining medical treatment for incompetent or disabled persons. Many of these patients never clearly expressed a desire to terminate their treatment, a circumstance the three leading right-to-die court rulings plainly illustrate. Claire Conroy generally resisted medical treatment but had not discussed the termination of artificially administered food and water. Yet the New Jersey Supreme Court viewed this as sufficient to authorize the removal of feeding tubes for the terminally ill retiree. Similarly, long before the injury causing his apparently irreversible coma, Paul Brophy indicated he did not want to be kept alive like Karen Ann Quinlan. The Massachusetts Supreme Court used this as part of the grounds for allowing Brophy's wife to end tube feeding. The famous *Quinlan* case, however, involved a father's request to remove a respirator, not a feeding tube, from a comatose young woman who had never expressed her desires about such life-sustaining treatment.[1]

As the first ruling of its kind, *Quinlan* generated widespread criticism from conservative Christian theologians, including Paul Ramsey of Princeton University. "The *Quinlan* case has gone a long way toward obliterating the distinction between voluntary and involuntary euthanasia," Ramsey wrote. "The court *imputed* to Karen a will to die; it did not discover it. Then the court permitted others also to impute a will to die to an uncomprehending patient and to act in behalf of that patient's privacy so construed. It does not matter *who* is the designated agent; *others* now have an extraordinary extralegal power to bring death." What troubled Ramsey most about the ruling was that Karen Ann Quinlan never chose to turn off the respirator. Instead, the court assumed she would want to die, in part "because the 'overwhelming majority' of us would want to do so" in a similar situation.[2]

The Emergence of Living Wills

Shortly after the *Quinlan* decision in 1976, and to some extent as a response to that widely publicized case, California became the first state to authorize living wills. Such legislation has been supported by pro-euthanasia and "patient's rights" groups. While right-to-life advocates generally opposed the California legislation, Ramsey reluctantly supported it.

Ramsey did not necessarily like the living-will concept, but he was heartened that the California law included *significant limits against voluntary euthanasia*. On the critical issue of involuntary euthanasia, he hoped that legislation allowing people to make final medical-treatment decisions in advance *for themselves* would discourage courts from giving that power to others acting on behalf of incompetent patients. "I do not know a better way than through our representatives in the state legislatures for a people to make known and effective its moral purposes in regard to the protection of life in the first and last of it," Ramsey affirmed. "Legislation is our last resort if I am correct in believing that the common law's ancient protection of life—against any private decision makers and against any consensus—is eroding."

At the time Ramsey acknowledged that his "political judgment differs from that voiced by the so-called pro-life movement, which has generally opposed such legislation." He admitted that future developments could readily prove his judgment incorrect.[3] More than a decade later, it remains unclear whether Ramsey's judgment was right or wrong. Thirty-eight states had enacted living-will statutes by the end of 1987. Some of those laws contain as many or more limitations against voluntary euthanasia as the California statute, but others do not. California itself has not loosened its law, contrary to the predictions of some opponents.

The verdict is even less clear on Ramsey's hopes that authorizing individuals to decide their own final medical treatment would keep others from usurping that power. Several living-will statutes run directly counter to those hopes by authorizing relatives to terminate medical treatment for incompetent individuals who have not signed a living will. Further, court rulings have continued to confer this power on relatives or guardians in absence of a living will, much as occurred in *Quinlan*. Yet the most extreme decisions of this type tend to come from states (such as Massachusetts, New Jersey, and New York) without living-will statutes. Perhaps, as Ramsey hoped, the option of living wills has discouraged judicial activism in other states.

Nevertheless, most right-to-life advocates continue to oppose living wills. As discussed in chapter 3, their primary concerns focus on provisions in living-will statutes specifying what treatment may be terminated and when. After examining the general terms of a living will, this chapter will suggest ways to tighten these key provisions within personalized documents. Means to request maximum medical treatment also appear.

Determining Treatment in Advance

Living wills, or advance treatment directives, involve a simple concept. Individuals may not be legally or physically able to choose their medical treatment during a potentially terminal illness. Living wills allow them to decide in advance and grant legal protection to health-care providers carrying out those decisions. Because the law traditionally does not allow people to make such decisions before the choice is at hand (in part because no one can anticipate all the considerations and factors that could arise at the time the decision is carried out), legislation is needed to make advance treatment directives enforceable.

The simple concept of a living will becomes confused at the point of putting it into practice because the thirty-eight state statutes authorizing living wills differ from one another. Unlike durable powers of attorney, where a simple concept is handled similarly throughout the nation, living wills display significant individual state differences that require consultation with a local attorney or other expert to understand and apply.

Most states recommend a form to follow in preparing a living will. The heart of each form consists of a declaration stating that life-sustaining procedures should be withheld or withdrawn in the event of a terminal condition. These documents can be quite brief, such as the following one-sentence "Declaration" suggested in Maine's Living Will Act:

> If I should have an incurable or irreversible condition
> that will cause my death within a short time, and if
> I am unable to participate in decisions regarding my
> medical treatment, I direct my attending physician
> to withhold or withdraw procedures that merely pro-
> long the dying process and are not necessary to my
> comfort or freedom from pain.

At the other extreme, the Utah statute recommends a six-paragraph "Directive to Physicians and Providers of Medical Services" that spells out key terms and conditions in the document.[4]

Actually, the length or specificity of a form living will makes little difference. Unless personal modifications are made in the state-supplied form, the *underlying statute* will control how and when the document applies. A more specific form document simply includes more of the definitions and terms from the statute in the living will itself; it does not change them.

The Maine Living Will Act illustrates this point. The statute underlying the brief "Declaration" defines "life-sustaining procedures" as "any medical procedure or intervention that, when administered to a qualified patient, will serve only to prolong the dying process and shall not include nutrition and hydration." Further, "'terminal condition' means an incurable or irreversible condition that, without the administration of life-sustaining procedures, will, in the opinion of the attending physician, result in death within a short time."[5] By executing their state's one-sentence form living will, Maine residents concurrently adopt these definitions. Thus, for example, even though the American Medical Association and many state statutes view artificially administered food and water as procedures that may be ended, a standard Maine living will denies that authority.

The Maine example demonstrates the importance of knowing precisely how a state's living will *statute* operates before executing a form document, and not relying simply on the words in the document. Even if the statutory provisions are satisfactory, it is prudent to include crucial terms in the actual document because the statute may change or the document may be used in another state where different provisions apply.

Comparing the flexibility of living wills with durable powers of attorney. This raises two limitations that make living wills less flexible than durable powers of attorney. First, all but three of the thirty-eight living-will states provide form documents that should be at least substantially followed, with four states (California, Georgia, Idaho, and Oregon) requiring that their form be precisely followed. This offers less leeway for crafting a personalized document than that allowed by durable powers of attorney. Second, while durable powers granted in one state are widely accepted across the country, only a handful of states recognize living wills from other states. In most instances when terminally ill patients are hospitalized out-of-state, a living will only serves as an indication of treatment preferences rather than a binding directive.

A Tightly Drawn Living Will Statute

The Maryland Life-Sustaining Procedures Act (which appears in Appendix 2 of this book) provides a good example of how a tightly drawn living-will statute operates. Maryland's form "Declaration" states:

> If at any time I should have an incurable injury, disease, or illness certified to be a terminal condition by two (2) physicians who have personally examined me, one (1) of whom shall be my attending physician, and the physicians have determined that my death is imminent and will occur whether or not life-sustaining procedures are utilized and where the application of such procedures would serve only to artificially prolong the dying process, I direct that such procedures be withheld or withdrawn, and that I be permitted to die naturally with only the administration of medication, the administration of food and water, and the performance of any medical procedure that is necessary to provide comfort care or alleviate pain. In the absence of my ability to give directions regarding the use of such life-sustaining procedures, it is my intention that this declaration shall be honored by my family and physician(s) as the final expression of my right to control my medical care and treatment.[6]

Maryland law allows any competent adult to execute a living will. The decision to do so must be voluntary, and it must be expressed in a signed, written document. These requirements are typical of most states, although a few permit a relative to execute a living will on behalf of a minor or an incompetent adult in certain situations. Paul Ramsey called this "the right to die once removed."[7] Most states require a patient to notify the attending physician if a living will has been signed, and provide that a copy should be included in the patient's medical records. Physicians are never required to comply with an advance treatment directive unless they know it exists. Every statute provides that written living wills must be signed in the presence of at least two adult witnesses.

Under Maryland law, a living will only takes effect when two prerequisites are satisfied. First, the patient must be unable to give directions regarding the use of life-sustaining procedures. This prerequisite, which applies in most places, allows patients who have signed living wills to continue making treatment decisions directly as long as they can. Second, two physicians (including the attending doctor) must certify that the patient is in a terminal condition. This is a common provision, although several states require certification only by the attending physician. Even where these prerequisites are satisfied, life-sustaining procedures cannot be ended under Maryland law if the patient is pregnant, an exception that appears in many living-will statutes.

Maryland narrowly defines "terminal condition" to mean "an incurable condition of a patient caused by injury, disease, or illness which to a reasonable degree of medical certainty makes death imminent and from which, despite the application of life-sustaining procedures, there can be no recovery."[8] This would not include most comatose patients, such as Karen Ann Quinlan and Paul Brophy, because they can survive indefinitely with treatment. Believing that living wills should do no more than let "the dying die," Ramsey favored this limitation: "A terminal condition should be understood in terms of impending death of the incurable. If anyone would have it otherwise . . . he opens the door to involuntary euthanasia."[9]

Most states do not require that death be imminent, however. For example, the Colorado law declares, " 'Terminal condition' means an incurable or irreversible condition for which the administration of life-sustaining procedures will serve only to postpone the moment of death."[10] This certainly includes persons in an irreversible coma or persistent vegetative state. Arkansas does not even require a terminal condition, but simply grants any person the right to refuse in advance "artificial, extraordinary, extreme or radical medical or surgical means or procedures calculated to prolong his life."[11]

State statutes also vary on the types of medical procedures covered by living wills. Over half of all living-will statutes (including the Maryland law) do not authorize the denial of nutrition and hydration (or sustenance), and nearly all states exempt procedures for comfort care and to alleviate pain. Except in those states where a form document must be precisely followed, anyone signing a living will may specify particular procedures that should never be terminated. Indeed, the Maryland statute expressly permits the addition of any provision to the form document not inconsistent with the statute. Alaska's form document goes a step further by including the option, "I _____ do/ _____ do not desire that nutrition or hydration (food and water) be provided by gastric tubes or intravenously if necessary."[12] Elsewhere, individuals must craft their own treatment provisions, some of which are suggested later in this chapter.

Exempting certain procedures does not change the basic nature of a living will. These documents provide advance authority for *ending* health care, not for requiring it. Thus, even if food and water are exempt, a living will still directs the termination of other life-sustaining procedures. Statutes in a few states, including Maryland, give individuals a parallel right to require in advance that all available life-sustaining medical procedures be provided in the event of a disabling and potentially terminal injury, disease, or illness. In most states, however, a "reverse" living will would only represent nonbinding evidence of a patient's preferences. C. Everett Koop and Edward R. Grant have criticized this "unidirectional" aspect of living wills.[13] Durable powers of attorney, in contrast, can direct a chosen agent to provide treatment rather than only to terminate it.

Finally, the Maryland statute contains several standard provisions, found in nearly all such laws, designed to facilitate the use of living wills. Physicians are required to implement a valid living will or promptly transfer a terminal patient to another physician. Life insurers are prohibited from declining coverage or refusing to pay benefits because of the execution or implementation of a living will. Any death pursuant to the statute is deemed to be by "natural process" and may not be considered a suicide or euthanasia. Persons may revoke their living wills any time (even when legally incompetent to sign one) by destroying or crossing out the document, by signing a written revocation, or (in certain circumstances) by simply saying so.

Drafting a Living Will

Analyzing Maryland's Life-Sustaining Procedures Act and comparing it with similar laws in other states reveals that there is more to a living will than meets the eye. A seemingly simple decision to sign a form living will automatically decides a complex host of other issues. People typically execute living wills to avoid prolonged and painful deaths hooked to costly machines offering no hope of recovery. Many signers never consider the issues of when treatment should end and if this should include food and water. Yet these issues are resolved in one way or another by law unless signers alter the form document. Thus, for example, signers of standard living wills in Texas authorize the termination of tube feeding in certain situations but those in neighboring Oklahoma do not—all without anything about the issue appearing in the documents themselves.

Except for those states where a prescribed form must be followed precisely, individuals can exert a measure of control over the terms of their living will by modifying the form document. This leeway is limited—and usually not as great as permitted in drafting durable powers of attorney—because most states require that form documents be substantially followed. Yet clear amendments to form documents generally are valid, especially where the amendment narrows the authority granted by statute rather than directs the termination of life-sustaining procedures beyond that authorized by law. Even if an amendment is not valid, the rest of the document may still stand, with the amendment serving as an expression of the signer's desires that may influence surrogate health-care decisions.

In every state where a form living will is supplied by statute (and this includes thirty-five of the thirty-eight states authorizing such documents), the prescribed form should be used as the basis for drafting. Amendments can then be made as desired. Yet no two prescribed forms are exactly alike. This makes it impossible to prepare standard amendments applicable to all living wills. Nevertheless, a few *key provisions*, designed for addition to standard living wills, appear below for consideration. When the amendment is inconsistent with the language of the form document, the form should be changed.

Defining the end. Perhaps the most controversial issue surrounding living wills remains the time of terminating medical treatment. Statutes differ significantly on this point, reflecting the sharp differences among ethicists and within the general public. Should living wills apply only when death is imminent or during any incurable illness? Because statutes differ and are vague on this point, persons signing living wills should consider including language specifying when to end treatment.

The following sample provision narrowly limits when medical procedures may end:

> I direct and desire that life-sustaining procedures be withheld or withdrawn under this document only when, to a reasonable degree of medical certainty, I am chronically and irreversibly incompetent, and in the final stage of a terminal injury, disease, or illness from which my death is imminent even with such treatment.[14]

The sample provision includes three basic qualifications for ending treatment. First, the patient must be unable to make decisions and unlikely ever to recover that ability. Second, the terminal condition must be in its final stage, which the statute defines, in part, as its "last stage" when the patient "is in the dying process and will die within a relatively short period of time."[15] Finally, death must be imminent with or without treatment, so that ending treatment simply lets the dying die without prolonging the dying process with futile procedures.

Qualifications of this type serve to clarify when the signer of a living will wants treatment to end rather than leaving it to the authorizing statute, which may be fatally vague. For example, one model statute authorizes the termination of any treatment serving only to prolong the process of dying. "The scope of the 'dying process,' however, is a highly subjective determination," Koop and Grant warn. "In the case of certain chronic ailments, such as Alzheimer's disease, the difficulty of caring for patients may exert subtle pressure to enlarge the temporal scope of the 'dying process.' "[16] This risk is reduced by amending a living will to specify, as much as possible, when treatment should end. Those specifics, of course, should reflect the wishes of the signer, and not those of the author of any statute, form document, or sample provision.

Food, water, and comfort care. Living-will statutes typically employ general terms to describe the types of life-sustaining medical procedures that may be terminated. This is inevitable. People often sign living wills long before they become terminally ill. No one can anticipate what treatments will be appropriate or available for a future illness. Therefore, living-will statutes give broad discretion to physicians in choosing which procedures to end. For example, the Montana Living Will Act allows doctors to end "any medical procedure or intervention that, when administered to [the] patient, will serve only to prolong the dying process."[17]

Although some ambiguity is unavoidable, some persons know in advance what medical procedures they *never* want discontinued. These procedures should appear in the living will, such as in the following sample provision:

> The procedures that may be withheld or withdrawn under this document do not include the administration of medication or sustenance (food and water), or the performance of any medical procedure deemed necessary to provide comfort care, or to alleviate pain.[18]

Most living-will statutes contain similar exemptions for comfort care and pain treatment, though many do not say so in the form document. Fewer exempt food and water.

These exemptions reflect widespread medical, ethical, and religious objections to terminating the named procedures. Those who oppose ending other procedures should not sign any living will unless it specifically identifies every type of treatment they always want to receive. This is a crucial safeguard even in states currently exempting those procedures from coverage under their living-will statutes because those laws may change or the document could be exercised in another state where the law differs.

Pregnancy exception. Pregnant women can give birth even after sustaining a terminal injury or lapsing into an irreversible coma. To protect the child in such situations, twenty-five of the thirty-eight living-will states provide by statute that advance treatment directives do not apply during pregnancy. This is usually not stated in form documents, however.

Women capable of bearing children may want to add precautionary language to their living wills to make sure this safeguard applies. The following provision from the Texas form living will serves as a model:

> If I have been diagnosed as pregnant and that diagnosis is known to my physician, this document shall have no force or effect during the course of my pregnancy.[19]

These sample provisions are not foolproof. Some states refuse to recognize amendments to form living wills. Also, health-care providers may treat all living-will patients alike without scrutinizing limitations added to individual documents. To minimize this risk, persons should tell their health-care providers, agents, and relatives about any special provisions added to their living wills. These people can then help insure those provisions are followed.

Living Wills Versus Durable Powers

Durable powers of attorney offer various advantages over

living wills for influencing future health-care decisions. As discussed in this chapter and in chapter 3, these advantages include the ability of the decision-maker named in a durable power of attorney to fashion treatment to the actual medical situation as it occurs, rather than having treatment governed by an inflexible written living will drafted prior to the illness. Also, directions in a living will may be less strictly followed than those given by a watchful agent acting under a durable power of attorney. But there are at least three situations where a living will may be preferable to a durable power of attorney.

A durable power of attorney is appropriate *only* if there is someone who can be trusted to make the "right" decisions. Many people do not have a relative or a friend who sufficiently shares their values and wishes to make life-and-death treatment decisions on their behalf. Even a like-minded relative or friend may not be willing or able to assume the heavy responsibility of making such decisions. Giving a durable power of attorney to someone likely to make wrong decisions can be worse than doing nothing. In some situations, a durable power of attorney can become little less than a license to kill. An individualized living will clearly reflecting personal treatment preferences, as inflexible as it may be, is preferable to a durable power of attorney entrusted to the wrong person.

Further, durable powers of attorney fail if none of the named agents are willing and able to serve when a disabling illness strikes. This could happen, for example, if a husband and wife name each other as agent and then one dies or both become disabled in a common accident. Living wills can serve as a back-up device for making health-care decisions in the event a durable power of attorney fails. Individuals in most states should be able to achieve this result by adding the following sample provision to their living wills:

> I direct and desire that this document only take effect
> if I have no agent willing and able to make health-
> care decisions for me under a durable power of
> attorney.

Of course, a durable power of attorney must also be executed for this provision to have any impact. Having *both* a durable power of attorney and a living will (and personalizing them both to reflect individual values and wishes) can provide double protection against unnamed persons or a court imposing unwanted treatment decisions.

Finally, a durable power of attorney is unnecessary for individuals who know in advance that they want maximum medical treatment in all situations. This choice leaves no decisions for a surrogate, and may be communicated by a written maximum treatment directive without naming an agent. Relatives, friends, and health-care providers should still be informed of the choice, however, and asked to respect it. Maximum treatment directives are discussed more fully in the following section.

Advance Requests for Maximum Treatment

Even though nearly every living-will statute disclaims any intention to allow euthanasia or suicide, some critics see a pro-death bias in these laws. "The living will is unidirectional in preserving the right to consent to medical treatment beyond the point of incompetency," Koop and Grant observed. "With the exception of a handful of statutes, living will laws do not permit patients to request that treatment be provided; they only permit patients to refuse treatment."[20]

Anyone may, however, sign a document requesting the application of all available medical procedures in the event of a disabling illness or injury. Although such directives are recognized by statute in only a few states, courts have ruled that surrogate decision-makers cannot terminate treatment contrary to a patient's known intentions.[21]

The Indiana Living Wills and Life-Prolonging Procedures Act contains a form declaration that can serve as a model maximum treatment directive.[22] With minor alterations, that form appears below. This document requests the use of all available medical procedures capable of extending life, including the administration of food and water. The optional language in brackets emphasizes that treatment should continue even after death is imminent regardless of cost.[23]

Life-Sustaining Procedures Declaration

I, _____ , being at least eighteen (18) years old and of sound mind, willfully and voluntarily make known my desire that if at any time I have an incurable injury, disease, or illness determined to be a terminal condition I request the use of all medical procedures, treatments, and interventions that would extend my life [or delay my death, without regard to my physical or mental diagnosis, condition, or prognosis, and without regard to financial cost]. This includes appropriate nutrition and hydration, the administration of medication, and the performance of all other medical procedures necessary to extend my life, to provide comfort care, or to alleviate pain.

In the absence of my ability to give directions regarding the use of life-sustaining procedures, it is my intention that this declaration be honored by my family and physician as the final expression of my legal right to request medical or surgical treatment and accept the consequences of the request.

I understand the full import of this declaration.

Signed _____ Date _____

Address _____

The declarant has been personally known to me, and I believe (him/her) to be of sound mind. I am competent and at least eighteen (18) years old.

Witness _____ Date _____

Witness _____ Date _____

Marshall Kapp, an advocate of maximum treatment directives, contends, "Just as proponents of death with dignity have living wills to effectuate their choice, those who embrace the 'sanctity of life' and its prolongation at all costs need a legally enforceable means to express their desire that all available medical resources be fully applied to them until the actual moment of their deaths."[24] Despite the endorsement of this option by the National Right to Life Committee, few states provide a legally enforceable means to request maximum treatment.[25] Nevertheless, a clear, effectively communicated request for maximum treatment should discourage courts, health-care providers, and surrogate decision-makers from terminating life-sustaining procedures.

Conclusions

The recent development and acceptance of living wills reflects a desire shared by many Americans to determine their final medical treatment in advance, while they are still able to do so. This began among persons who wanted to avoid futile treatment, especially following the publicity surrounding Karen Ann Quinlan and other comatose or terminally ill patients artificially kept alive without hope of recovery. Interest later spread to people wanting to assure receiving some or all types of treatment, especially tube feeding, in response to court decisions allowing surrogate decision-makers to end health care for incompetent patients.

Living wills remain inflexible devices at best. Many populous states, particularly in the Northeast, do not officially recognize such documents. Most other states prescribe form documents that must be at least substantially followed. Only a few states expressly authorize individuals to request maximum treatment in advance.

Despite these limitations, advance directives either requesting or refusing treatment understandably appeal to many people. Before signing any document, however, individuals should carefully consider what types of treatment they do and do not want, and when. Sincerely held personal beliefs on these matters should appear in these documents whenever possible. Living wills were intended to carry out personal desires, not to ride roughshod over them. They should increase a patient's peace of mind when confined to a hospital bed—not be a source of increased concern.

Chapter 8, Notes

1. *In re Conroy*, 98 N.J. 321, 486 A.2d 1209, 1218, 1242-43 (1985); *Brophy v. New England Sinai Hospital*, 398 Mass. 417, 497 N.E.2d 626, 632 n. 22 (1986); and *In re Quinlan* 70 N.J. 10, 355 A.2d 647, 664 (1976), *cert. denied sub nom. Garger v. New Jersey*, 429 U.S. 922 (1976); and Paul

Ramsey, *Ethics at the Edges of Life: Medical and Legal Intersections* (New Haven, Conn.: Yale University Press, 1978), 270.

2. Ramsey, *Ethics*, 293-94.
3. Ibid., 329-30.
4. *Me. Rev. Stat.* tit. 22, sec. 2922(4); and *Utah Code Ann.* sec. 75-2-1104.
5. *Me. Rev. Stat.* tit. 22, sec. 2921 (4) and (8).
6. *Md. Health General Code* Ann. sec. 5-602(c)(1).
7. Ramsey, *Ethics*, 318.
8. *Md. Health General Code* Ann. sec. 5-601(c).
9. Ramsey, *Ethics*, 326-27.
10. *Colo. Rev. Stat.* sec. 15-18-103(10).
11. *Ark. Stat. Ann.* sec. 82-3801.
12. *Alaska Stat.* sec. 18.12.010.
13. C. Everett Koop and Edward R. Grant, "The 'Small Beginnings' of Euthanasia: Examining the Erosion in Legal Prohibitions Against Mercy-Killing," *Notre Dame Journal of Law, Ethics & Public Policy* 2 (1986):600.
14. This provision is based on language in a 1987 Oklahoma statute, endorsed by the National Right to Life Committee, designed to restrict when certain medical procedures may be discontinued. 63 *Ok. Rev. Stat.* sec. 3080.4; and Dave Andrusko, "Oklahoma Food & Water Bill Major Pro-Life Breakthrough," *National Right to Life News,* 18 June 1987, 1.
15. 63 *Ok. Rev. Stat.* sec 3081.2.
16. Koop and Grant, "'Small Beginnings,'" 613.
17. *Mont. Rev. Code* Ann. sec. 50-9-102(4).
18. This sample provision closely tracks language in Utah's form living will. *Utah Code Ann.* sec. 75-2-1104(4).
19. *Tex. Stat. Ann.* art. 4590h, sec. 3(d).
20. Koop and Grant, "'Small Beginnings,'" 600.
21. *E.g., In re Conroy,* 486 A.2d at 1232.
22. *Ind. Code* sec. 16-8-11-12.
23. This optional language is drawn from a sample maximum treatment directive suggested in a 1982 *American Journal of Medicine* article by Marshall B. Kapp of Wayne State University.
24. Marshall B. Kapp, "Responses to the Living Will Furor: Directives for Maximum Care," *The American Journal of Medicine* 72 (1982):856-57.
25. David N. O'Steen, "Restoring the Presumption to Treat," *National Right to Life News,* 27 March 1986, 10.

Chapter 9

Hospice Care and Ministry to the Elderly:
Making Life Worth Living

"*I*f the sting of death is sin, the sting of dying is solitude,"
writes ethicist Paul Ramsey. "Desertion is more choking
than death, and more feared. The chief problem of the dying
is how not to die alone."[1] In response to this, a new concept
of care has been developing since the 1960s. It restores to
medical practice the art of relationship, which Dr. Rob Roy
MacGregor emphasized in chapter 1. And it relies very little—if
at all—on advanced technology. Its main objectives are to
control pain, provide companionship, assist terminal patients
and families in preparing for death, and offer bereavement care
for the family after death occurs.

The concept is *hospice*, a term derived from the Latin
word for "hospitality." Originally it meant a lodging for travel-
ers. Today, instead of being a particular place, hospice is a
program of care that may take place in the patient's home, in
or adjacent to a regular hospital, or in a separate in-patient
facility. A team of professionals works closely with the family
to offer care tailored to the needs and desires of each individual
patient.

173

Hospice nurse Roberta Paige of Portsmouth, Virginia, explains the hospice philosophy: "The modern hospice is a rest stop for individuals who are traveling from this life to the next. The intent is to help prepare the individual for the crossing over. . . . Hospice care is reflective of the value system that says we are of value because of who we are and by virtue of the fact that we are human; our value is not determined by what we can do."

Modern hospice care originated in England in 1967, when Dr. Cicely Saunders opened St. Christopher's in London. The first U. S. hospice program patterned after St. Christopher's began in 1974 in New Haven, Connecticut, and there are currently more than seventeen hundred hospices in the United States, according to the National Hospice Organization in Arlington, Virginia. Approximately one-third are run by religious organizations, and spiritual care is an integral part of every hospice program.

Hospice offers patients and their families an important choice when they confront a terminal illness. Though not a panacea, it appears increasingly to be a solution that satisfies everyone involved with the patient, and best of all, minimizes the patient's own suffering. An example of the hospice concept was included in the Introduction to this book. Francis and Edith Schaeffer made the difficult decision to keep him off life-support machines at the end of his fight with cancer. He returned home to familiar surroundings that included music, a garden, and caring friends and family. There he died, in the company of people he loved and away from the sterility and intrusions of hospital care.

Significantly, the people involved in providing hospice care have little in common with the euthanasia movement. The two initiatives have coexisted in an uneasy tension for the past two decades. Many observers fervently hope the spread of hospice care and improvements in pain control will render powerless the arguments for euthanasia. Robert Fulton and Greg Owen point out, "In a world in which technology threatens to undermine our sense of worth and meaning, hospice has appeared with the promise of not only easing the course for those who must die, but also of restoring the fundamental familial and religious ideals that have nourished our civilization."[2]

Making life worth living is an important goal for all elderly or incapacitated people, not just people who are terminally ill. After a discussion of hospice care, including its ethical and spiritual significance, this chapter will conclude with descriptions of church and community-based programs that stimulate and involve the elderly in ongoing activities. As Surgeon General Koop has reminded us, how we define their "quality of life" reflects the moral quality of our own lives. Abandonment and neglect are feared by the elderly as well as by the dying in our society. We need to learn how to lift those threats from the lives of our most vulnerable citizens, or philosophical opposition to euthanasia will ring hollow indeed.

What Is Hospice Care?

In 1947, Dame Cicely Saunders met a patient on her rounds as a social worker in England. The patient was a Jewish man from Warsaw, David Tasma, and he did not know he was dying. Saunders knew, and she eventually told him. She recalls, "The foundation of St. Christopher's is how we coped with that truth together." What David Tasma needed most of all, Saunders discerned, was a sense of belonging and meaningfulness. "David needed peace from distress to sort out who he was, to find how he could gather the scattered fragments of what looked an unfulfilled life somehow into a whole at its ending."[3]

That sort of care was not available through Britain's National Health Service, so Saunders embarked on a new project to offer terminal care that ministered to the emotions and the soul as well as the body. Saunders had been trained as a nurse. She became a medical social worker and eventually a physician because of her interest in the terminally ill. Saunders is widely recognized for her pioneering work to control the pain of terminal cancer patients.

St. Christopher's, the hospice Saunders started, is funded in part by Britain's health service. It provides inpatient care, teams of professionals for home-based care, and bereavement assistance. It is a major center for education, training, and research on the hospice concept of care. Anne Munley, an American sociologist and Roman Catholic nun, explains the uniqueness of hospice care developed by Saunders:

> Rather than being anti-technological, the hospice seeks to use technology in the service of the dying by blending expert methods of pain and symptom control with human warmth, understanding, and the interpersonal support known as 'bonding.' Rather than being anti-scientific, the hospice seeks to unite the knowledge that flows from science with the openness to mystery that springs from faith and the compassion that arises from caring. Rather than being anti-institutional, the hospice seeks to provide highly personalized care of the dying in institutional settings as well as on patient and family turf in the home. Rather than being anti-specialization, the hospice seeks to meld the benefits of specialization with an emphasis on a team approach that recognizes the value of role flexibility: in a hospice, a social worker may carry a tray, a maintenance worker may comfort a patient, and a physician may promise a prayer.[4]

The majority of hospice patients are in the advanced stages of cancer, and many suffer from serious pain. Preventing pain before it begins, rather than relieving it on demand, is one of the main features setting hospice care apart from routine hospitalization. Hospice workers recognize that pain is made worse by anxiety or the anticipation of more pain. Saunders, in her research on pain alleviation, found that pain can best be controlled by providing medication at regular intervals, such as every four hours. Special care is given to assure the patient will be as alert and active as possible.

Hospice care patterned after the St. Christopher's approach came to the United States in 1974, when a hospice in New Haven, Connecticut, opened its doors. A main difference between the British program and its counterpart in America is funding. The United States has no comprehensive national health service, and funding for most of the nation's hospice programs comes from private sources. Increasingly, hospice care qualifies for insurance coverage and Medicare benefits. Health-care providers, community planners, and insurance officials are searching for ways to integrate already-existing services so hospice care can be made available to all who need and want it.

Roberta Paige, who established the first hospice program based in a U. S. hospital in the mid-1970s, describes one of the distinctives of hospice care: "Hospice care is not appropriate for every terminal patient. It is not appropriate for the person who wants everything done, including experimental medication and treatments. The person most likely to benefit is the one who is in desperate need of relief from a distressing symptom. Individuals in emotional turmoil and in spiritual distress have been greatly helped by hospice care. Individuals who need an advocate in the [health-care] system, particularly people living alone, seem very appreciative of hospice care."

How a Hospice Program Works

At the fifteen-bed inpatient building of Hospice of Northern Virginia, the sterile, high-tech, scrubbed-white feel of a hospital is entirely absent. An elderly patient's bed is wheeled into the hallway for a change of scene, and a visitor arrives with a white toy poodle. The dog leaps eagerly into the patient's lap, greeting an old friend. In the kitchen, family members can prepare special treats for ailing loved ones. A patient lounge offers the warmth of a living room, with bay windows, mini-blinds, lemon-yellow walls, attractive watercolors, and inviting sofas. The chapel is equipped with an altar, chairs, and a wide selection of devotional reading material.

In the library, a team meeting is under way. Interdisciplinary teams are the key to individualized, flexible hospice care which is available to every patient twenty-four hours a day, seven days a week. Four Northern Virginia teams are responsible for different geographic regions of the Washington, D. C., suburbs, and each includes a physician, nurse, medical social worker, bereavement counselor, and at least one volunteer. A full-time chaplain, the Rev. Jeanne Brenneis, assists all four teams in meeting the spiritual needs of their patients.

At the weekly team meeting, the needs and status of approximately twenty patients are reviewed. An AIDS patient, newly baptized by the hospice chaplain, wants to get in touch with other Christians. Concerns are raised about a deceased patient's sister who refused to visit the funeral home. Hospice follow-up includes seeing the family through its initial grief. One patient, a former top executive, had vented his anger and discomfort at two team members. The team agrees to order a more comfortable, adjustable bed for his home. Like most patients admitted to hospice care, he has a prognosis of six months or less to live.

Hospice of Northern Virginia cares for between eighty and one hundred terminal patients at a time, and most remain at home with a family member providing primary care. A patient may enter the inpatient facility when he or she is gravely ill or needs special nursing attention. Most inpatient residents stay for one or two weeks, then are discharged back to their homes. Training and supporting family members through an often excruciating life crisis is a focus of hospice care. To Peggy Beckman, a nurse who directs one of Northern Virginia's four teams, hospice care is "the most rewarding and satisfying work I've ever been involved with. It can be sad and it's certainly stressful," she adds. Dying, in Beckman's view, "has to be a frightening experience, and so many people go through it scared and alone. Hospice work is a wonderful way to say,

'I'm going to walk that road with you' and to be able to relieve someone of that fear."

Paige gives the following description of what this can mean in the lives of two patients:

> One patient told me that he became very upset when the cleaning man went by with his bags of trash. He felt that all that he was to become was a useless commodity in a plastic wrapping. He mentioned dispersing his wife's ashes at sea and commented on how unsettling it was to think of her as a pile of ashes. He had a deep need to see some meaning and purpose in his life. He was very interested in hearing my thoughts on God and man and an after-life.
>
> A retarded patient who lived alone in a single room looked at me and said, "I look like a monster, don't I?" I winced, because he was very unpleasant to look at; the whites of his eyes were red. I knew, though, that this was a patient who desperately needed love and acceptance. Love took the form of the chaplain going to his hotel room and making nutritious, appetizing meals. Love meant taking him for a ride in a wheelchair to other parts of the hospital so he could listen to some piano music or attend a tea party. The hospice team and the hospital staff became his family. His memorial service was held in the hospital's chapel.

The daily experience of hospice teams appears to be contributing a deeper understanding of death and our "control" over our circumstances. Chaplain Brenneis notes, "We joke about 'God's prognosis,' because the patient we think is going to be with us for a couple weeks lives for a year, and the one we think has lots of time suddenly declines very fast. Nobody knows when he or she is going to die, and that is one of the hardest and most frustrating things a patient and family have to deal with."

In many cases, patients with unfinished business or an important unfulfilled goal (such as seeing a new grandchild) stay alive until they feel a sense of completion or release. Paige recalls, "One husband could not accept the fact that his wife was dying. She lingered and lingered until one day he came in and said, 'I emptied out your drawers.' She died within twenty-four hours. I believe she was waiting to die until he could release her."

Hospice personnel sometimes see the worst in human nature when a family rejects a dying member. Jo Turner, with Hospice of Northern Virginia, remembers, "One young woman wanted to die at home more than anything else in the world. But her husband had already had a woman move in with him. He didn't want his wife home, obviously. She would call me, crying. I asked the husband to come in to talk about it, and he brought the other woman in with him. He stalled long enough for his wife to die, and I hurt for her terribly."

On many occasions, however, the best of human nature and the transcendent grace of God are evident. Paige reminisces about "a very angry young man" she treated:

> My initial contact with him was when he threw a urinal across the room. He hated the hospital and was angry about his diagnosis. He had severe pain and learned that he was sterile because of chemotherapy and could not father any children. He then became paralyzed from the waist down.

> The hospice team controlled his pain and arranged for him to give a guitar concert to the staff. On steaming hot days, the chaplain would visit him in his apartment, bringing the patient's favorite flavor of ice cream. The patient received a lot of love, and in the process learned something about Jesus. He made Jesus Lord of his life and spent his last days praying for his roommates in the hospital, rejoicing when they seemed to be getting better. He was and

remains an inspiration to me of what the Spirit of God can do in and through a person.

Integrating Spiritual and Medical Care

Affirming a relationship with God may be a terminal patient's most important task, Chaplain Brenneis has found. An AIDS patient in Northern Virginia provides a case in point. He was the son of a Baptist clergyman, and he had never been baptized. He decided during the course of his illness that God was calling him to a visible sign of commitment through baptism. Brenneis recalls, "In early September I baptized him right here in the inpatient unit. His sister and brother-in-law came here for it, as well as his mother, home care nurse, and social worker. He has his baptism certificate at home, framed, on a coffee table in front of the couch where he spends most of his time. He says it has made his life much better. He is more at peace, he has repented, and feels washed and clean. He would love to belong to a church now, but cannot go out."

Brenneis's role is a difficult one, and she often hears the despairing refrain, "I just wish it were over. I'm tired of this." She gently reminds patients of the good things in life that remain for them to enjoy. "I pray with people regularly, giving thanks for this day and for all the signs of God's love in it. In my counseling, I try to nudge people to see that even in the despair of knowing that your life is ending, there are bright spots—very bright spots. There are relationships they are not finished with, children and grandchildren. We try to help people be fully alive while they are dying—to the very end."

Keen attention to spiritual needs is an essential component of hospice care. At the same time, as we have seen in previous chapters, the church may be the most well-equipped institution to begin helping society at large deal with the realities of death in a high-tech age. In at least one case, church ministry and hospice care have merged to make this a reality. In East Point, Georgia, Southwest Christian Church finances a hospice program through the generosity of its nine-hundred-member congregation. The hospice program's 1988 budget totaled $373,000. And because of the church's commitment to Southwest Christian Hospice, no fee is charged for patient care.

A description of how this hospice program met the needs of one elderly cancer patient illustrates the concept. Former director Dale Fjeran and current director Janice Weaver, a registered nurse, describe a real patient using a fictitious name, Mrs. Johnson.

Mrs. Johnson, at age seventy-six, had been diagnosed with cancer of the colon and liver one year before referral to hospice care. Surgery and chemotherapy had failed to stop the disease from spreading throughout her body. She left her hometown and moved in with her son and granddaughter. At an initial meeting with hospice personnel at Southwest Christian Hospice, Mrs. Johnson was weak and in pain. The nurse who interviewed her detected that she was willing to take medication only when her pain became unbearable.

She received assistance from three older sisters who came to her son's home each weekend to clean and cook, but she needed attention during the weekdays when her son worked and her granddaughter was in school. The hospice team assigned to Mrs. Johnson consisted of three volunteers, including a nurse. They visited regularly, ran errands, shampooed Mrs. Johnson's hair, and simply stayed with her while other family members took a much-needed break. As she grew weaker, she became unable to swallow pain medication, so the nurse taught family members how to give injections.

Fjeran and Weaver write, "Another need that hospice was able to meet for Mrs. Johnson was her desire for pastoral visits for Bible reading and prayer. Since she had not been in our area long, she had not established a church home although she professed an active Christian faith."[5]

When Mrs. Johnson slipped into a coma, the family asked a hospice representative to stay in the home until she died. A nurse stayed, encouraging the family to remain by Mrs. Johnson's side and assure her that they loved her. She died peacefully in her bed, with her three sisters, children, and one grandchild with her.[6]

Southwest's hospice program began in 1983, and one year later the state of Georgia established state guidelines for licensed hospice programs. The state requires certain personnel, including a medical director, nurse, social worker, and counselor. Written policies and procedures, twenty-four-hour-a-day availability, and some provision for inpatient care are required. Southwest Christian Church established a governing body for the hospice out of its own pool of trustees. Sixteen hospice staff members are paid for their work, and sixty-five volunteers are drawn from the congregation.

Fjeran and Weaver point out that hospice care may evolve naturally out of existing church ministries:

> Your church may already have a ministry of caring for members who are sick at home; with some broadening, your ministry can become a hospice ministry. . . . The size of a congregation is a secondary consideration to the starting of a hospice program. The desire to serve is vital. Granted, congregations that are few in number would find it difficult to undertake such a ministry on their own. But that would not preclude them from forming a consortium of churches in the area that would have a similar interest to launch such a program.[7]

Hospice and Euthanasia

The hospice solution addresses many of the medical realities discussed in chapter 1, offering an alternative to aggressive hospital measures that may prolong a patient's dying. It reintroduces the concept of family involvement, as well as teamwork among physician, nurse, chaplain, and patient. Its emphasis on pain prevention—or palliative care—offers tremendous psychological reassurance to dying people fearing pain and abandonment. It is considerably less expensive than hospitalization, and in some cases the financial burden is borne at least in part by members of a larger network, such as a church.

But how does the hospice concept fit in with the social realities and popular opinion examined in chapter 2? Will a steady drumbeat on behalf of the "right to die" undermine hospice as a measure most Americans will enthusiastically support? That does not appear to be the case. Hospice has enjoyed tremendous popularity in the press and growing acceptance within the traditional health-care field.

Howard Kleckner, a cancer physician at Kaiser-Permanente Medical Center in Hayward, California, admits his initial reluctance about hospice care. "After just completing the training program at the University aimed at saving cancer patients by aggressive treatment, I was hardly prepared for the idea of a place for patients to die," he writes.[8] After a year, however, some of Kleckner's patients were beginning to fail. They were experiencing symptoms of terminal illness that chemotherapy could not help, and family members approached him with questions about what to do.

When the Kaiser-Hayward Hospice Unit opened, Kleckner saw it as an ideal solution. "Hospice has expanded my capabilities as a physician to provide a more decent and humane service to a suffering patient. It is a humbling experience to be a physician; society has great expectations of a doctor's skills, but reality dictates their limits very plainly. These limits have been expanded by the concept of hospice—how far depends on how much effort we as physicians and health providers are willing to put forth."[9]

Where hospice meets the euthanasia movement, however, the reception is less enthusiastic. The writings of the right-to-die activists tend to pay scant attention to hospice, dismissing it as a solution for only a few terminal cancer patients. At the same time, writers such as Derek Humphry attempt to embrace the concept as being compatible with euthanasia. Humphry writes, "Put bluntly, hospice makes the best of a bad job and they do so with great skill and love. The euthanasia movement supports their work. . . . We do not feel there is any cross purpose between euthanasia and hospice; both are appropriate to different people, with different values."[10]

Promoters of voluntary suicide and active euthanasia emphasize individual choice and autonomy, but they concede, "almost all euthanasists would probably resist the idea of dying in a hospice."[11] The difference between the two movements appears to originate in different spiritual orientations. Humphry and Wickett note in their book, *The Right to Die*, that hospice workers who are religiously motivated are much more likely to oppose euthanasia:

> On the West Coast of America, where the major religions are less entrenched than in more conservative or orthodox areas, hospice organizations tend to be more receptive to euthanasia groups, exchanging speakers at conferences and referring patients to each other. In quite a few instances, area leaders of the hospice movement will also be active members of the Hemlock Society. East Coast hospice groups tend to be less cooperative, while British hospice is disapproving of all euthanasia societies.[12]

Hospice founder Cicely Saunders's own opposition to euthanasia is long-standing and eloquent. In a 1980 article, she wrote, "When someone asks for euthanasia or turns to suicide, I believe in almost every case someone, or society as a whole, has failed that person. To suggest that such an act should be legalized is to offer a negative and dangerous answer to problems which should be solved by better means."[13]

But what about the terminal patient who says he wants to "end it all" due to discomfort, despair, or neglect by family members? Hospice personnel typically cope with this in a way that resolutely resists death as a solution. Peggy Beckman, at Hospice of Northern Virginia, says, "The first thing we have to let them know up front is that this is not something we can help them accomplish. Some families have the idea that hospice is a place that will help you die. We have to clear up those misconceptions. What I have found, when I have had to deal with this personally with patients, is that most of it comes down to fear of what they are going to suffer. If you reassure them that you are here to see that they do not suffer, it helps." Hospice of Northern Virginia has seen four suicides out of thousands of patients in its first ten years of operation.

Paige notes, "Hospice patients don't tend to request assistance in suicide because they do not feel abandoned nor do they feel that they are a burden. They know that every effort will be made to control their symptoms."

Beyond the dilemma of the individual patient, Saunders is greatly concerned about the impact euthanasia would have on elderly people as a group and society as a whole: "The best way to live on is to remain as active as possible and to receive the respect of others; the worst way is to be told continually how sad and undignified old age can be and how we should be free to ask to be rid of it." Even though hospice care does not reach every terminal patient directly, its contribution to research and instruction on aspects of pain, relationships, and fulfillment for the dying must be recognized, she insists. Legalized euthanasia, on the other hand, would undermine confidence and care for countless people: "I believe that to make voluntary euthanasia or assisted suicide lawful would be an irresponsible act, hindering help, pressuring the vulnerable and abrogating our true respect and responsibility to the frail, the old and the dying."[14]

In America, similar reasoning from many hospice proponents holds the euthanasia philosophy at bay. Anne Munley argues, "As far as the hospice is concerned, legalization of euthanasia would be nothing more than a cheap, expedient solution to the problem of terminal care, at the expense of the patient's best welfare. . . . Rather than being a 'foot in the door' for euthanasia, the hospice movement can be a powerful force for undercutting a movement for active euthanasia."[15]

Hospice, Living Wills, and Durable Powers of Attorney

How does hospice care mesh with living wills and durable powers of attorney, the other alternatives discussed in this section? Because care is geared specifically to terminally ill patients with six months or fewer to live, it is not an all-encompassing solution to the health-care dilemmas some individuals inevitably face. Entry into hospice care is a decision made by a patient, family member, or designated surrogate when a terminal illness or condition is deemed to be beyond the reach of modern medicine and hospitalization. It is not a substitute for making decisions in advance about the treatment or nontreatment a person desires, nor is it a substitute for appointing an attorney-in-fact for health-care decisions.

Advance decisions may be crucial for carrying out the wishes of a patient who desires hospice care but becomes unable to make a legally binding choice. Further, the decision to enter hospice care may be less agonizing for the family of an incompetent patient who has made his wishes known through an advance treatment directive. And choosing a surrogate decision-maker can relieve tension over who should take responsibility for contacting a hospice program on behalf of an incapacitated loved one.

The National Hospice Organization addresses these issues. It advises, "Hospices should have written policies concerning who should make decisions on behalf of patients who are incapable of making their own decisions, and these policies should reflect state statutes and court decisions governing the jurisdiction in which the hospice is located."[16] Generally hospice programs incorporate family members into the day-to-day decisions and details of comfort and care for terminal patients. However, the National Hospice Organization notes, "unless there is a state law clearly giving family members the right to consent (or refuse consent) for medical care, a decision called into question . . . may not be binding. It is for this reason that written directives from the patient are greatly to be preferred."[17]

Hospice care is dedicated to preserving as much patient autonomy as possible, so the National Hospice Organization states, "To the extent possible, it is important for the patient to maintain control of decision-making for legal and ethical reasons as well as for the patient's medical and psychological well-being."[18]

As noted in chapter 7, many living-will statutes exempt comfort care and pain alleviation—the two main goals of hospice—from the treatments that may be withheld or withdrawn. So in the context of a hospice program, nurses, patients, and family members work closely together to determine the appropriate course of care and treatment. In most cases, hospice patients have decided already to discontinue extraordinary treatment; in effect, their living will, if they had one, is implemented when they enter the hospice program.

However, the National Hospice Organization points out that some hospice procedures fall into uncharted territory with regard to prolonging life. The organization states, "A major weakness of a natural death act as applied in hospice care is that it is not always clear whether a proposed procedure constitutes 'extraordinary treatment'—or a medical intervention that would unnecessarily prolong the patient's dying—or whether it is merely supportive, palliative care."[19] To help clarify the goal of hospice care ahead of time, Janice Weaver of Southwest Christian Hospice says new patients must sign a form saying they understand that hospice personnel will not attempt to resuscitate them if, for example, they suffer a heart attack.

It is not enough for a person to decide in advance that they will opt for hospice care in the event of a terminal illness. Hospice is an important alternative, but the need for written documents stating who will decide and what should be decided remains. Even after the patient is admitted to hospice care, living wills and durable powers of attorney can serve the patient's best interests by making his or her desires clear despite the loss of ability to communicate.

The National Hospice Organization, based in Arlington, Virginia, represents many of the nation's hospice programs and offers further information about hospice care and provides referrals to available community services.[20] The organization summarizes the hospice philosophy this way:

The purpose of hospice is to provide support and care for people in the final phase of a terminal disease so that they can live as fully and comfortably as possible. Hospice affirms life and regards dying as a normal process. Hospice neither hastens nor postpones death. Hospice believes that through personalized services and a caring community, patients and families can attain the necessary preparation for a death that is satisfactory to them.

Preemptive Acts: How Some Churches Are Restoring Respect for the Elderly

Beyond hospice care, there is a broader need in society to recognize and meet the challenges of a growing elderly population. Restoring respect, building community awareness, and promoting cross-generational activities and ministry opportunities are all part of this bigger picture. In the Tony Award-winning Broadway play, "I'm Not Rappaport," an elderly man in Central Park concocts a fantasy world that gets him into all sorts of trouble. His daughter finally confronts him with two choices: He can enter a home for the elderly or move into her home in the distant suburbs. Attached to his favorite park bench and elderly companions, the old man protests that these choices amount to "kindergarten" or "Siberia."

Is there any way for society to offer a more palatable alternative? Sociologist David Moberg believes the church holds the key: "Organized religion is the best institutional friend that the elderly have ever had."[21] That does not mean churches are doing all they can do; but the potential clearly exists for churches and other religious organizations to develop an entirely new context for making life worth living among the elderly, the handicapped, and the terminally ill.

This book has considered critical issues of health care choices which need to be thought through by everyone. The church plays an important part in that process by offering an ethical and biblical context for determining what is appropriate and what is not. The church also can make a critical difference in assisting the elderly and their families to make sound choices about the retirement years. Tim Stafford, writing in *Christianity Today*, notes, "If seniors opt out of the challenges of the coming century, if they retire into senior hedonism and toss away a quarter of their adult life, we will lose our wisest, most experienced leaders before their time. And if the church neglects the elderly, overlooking their needs and their potential because we are so used to focusing on young families, we will miss a key opportunity. In a rapidly increasing sense, the old are our future."[22]

Churches across the country are beginning to recognize this and do something about it. At St. John's Lutheran Church in Stamford, Connecticut, a full-time staff position for ministry to seniors was established in 1983. Jean E. Thompson, director of Life Care Ministry at the church, describes the scope of the program and profiles the elderly there, who constitute nearly one-fifth of the congregation: "Our goal is to visit each elderly family unit at least twice a year. With most people the contact is much more frequent than that. We visit one woman every week as part of her hospital discharge plan to alleviate depression," Thompson writes. "Visits help to ease loneliness, maintain contact with the church family, cement bonds of friendship, and keep the church familiar with individual needs."[23]

The over-sixty-five population at St. John's church is healthy and active, with 90 percent of them competent to perform the tasks of daily living. More than half are married, well over three-fourths live in their own homes, and most are well educated and have sufficient income. Two individuals are in nursing homes, four live in apartments where they are assisted in some tasks, and eight live with family members.

Beyond regular visits, trained volunteers offer a variety of services, including transportation, meal preparation, shopping, and delivering tapes of Sunday worship services. They help prepare for monthly seniors' meetings, which include a meal and often a program or trip. Four of the over-sixty-five set serve on an advisory board, along with Thompson and St. John's pastor, to plan activities. The seniors give as well as receive: In 1985, the club marked the three-hundredth anniversary of composer J. S. Bach by sponsoring a Sunday covered-dish luncheon and concert for the entire congregation.

Spiritual as well as social needs are addressed. Devotions are offered at each meeting, Bible studies and special services are regularly featured, and a monthly newsletter keeps club members informed. The seniors even organized an adult class to meet during Vacation Bible School one year. A number of the club's participants want to take on a mission or service project as well.

St. John's Life Care program reaches out to other age groups in the church. Seminars for children of aging parents address concerns about health, behavior changes, and available resources. Even youth programs and Sunday school classes have considered aspects of aging. Children have been encouraged to play games that promote understanding and sensitivity toward the elderly, and church youth organize leaf-raking sessions in the fall to help elderly members.

The results of Life Care Ministry speak for its success. Thompson writes, "Older adults at St. John's are a visible and viable component of the church's life. The elderly are feeling positive about themselves and enjoy the personal attention by a member of the church staff. Others in the congregation are beginning to be aware of the seniors as an active, talented, intelligent and caring group of people."[24]

Programs such as this are beginning to take shape at many churches across America. By making life worth living for the elderly while they remain alert, active, and involved, churches cultivate a new perspective on aging. When the elderly do become ill or incapacitated, their church friends and ministers will know and love them as individuals. These enhanced relationships may be especially important when the time comes for an elderly person to designate a surrogate decision-maker. They may be enabled to do so with confidence that they are not viewed as aliens abandoned by church people in their rush to serve only the youth, the young families, and the singles.

Conclusions

Defeating euthanasia as a movement and an increasingly acceptable option is not the point or purpose of hospice care for the dying or ministry to the elderly. These positive approaches are motivated instead by the indisputable worth and dignity of human beings, no matter what their physical condition. The day-to-day concerns of hospice providers and church ministries to the elderly have much more to do with compassion and care than with active opposition to an organized pro-euthanasia movement. But unsung efforts to honor the elderly and respect those who are dying could have a significant impact on how society views this rapidly growing population group.

Euthanasia is virtually irrelevant in circles where the elderly have high self-esteem, a sense of purpose, and a close community. As these circles widen and multiply nationwide through the work of churches and other institutions dedicated to preserving life from start to finish, the grip of the appeal euthanasia holds may slowly be loosened. Meanwhile, finding antidotes to the sting of loneliness threatening the elderly and eventually ourselves is a task that merits avid and careful attention.

Chapter 9, Notes

1. Paul Ramsey, *The Patient as Person* (New Haven, Conn.: Yale University Press, 1970), 134.

2. Robert Fulton and Greg Owen, "Hospice in the United States," in *Hospice: The Living Idea* (London: Edward Arnold Publishers, 1981), 11.

3. Dame Cicely Saunders, "The Founding Philosophy," in *Hospice*, 44.

4. Anne Munley, *The Hospice Alternative* (New York: Basic Books, Inc., 1983), 30.

5. Dale R. Fjeran and Janice Weaver, "Hospice," in *Special Ministries for Caring Churches*, ed. Robert E. Korth (Cincinnati: Standard Publishing, 1986), 115.

6. Ibid.

7. Ibid., 117, 120.

8. Howard Kleckner, "From the Physicians' View," in *Hospice Pilot Project Report* by Norman T. Walter (Hayward, Calif.: Kaiser-Permanente Medical Center, 1979), 123.

9. Ibid., 124.

10. Derek Humphry, "The Case for Rational Suicide," *The Euthanasia Review*, Fall 1986, 174.

11. Derek Humphry and Ann Wickett, *The Right to Die: Understanding Euthanasia* (New York: Harper & Row, 1986), 181.

12. Ibid., 186.

13. Cicely Saunders, "Caring to the End," *Nursing Mirror*, 4 September 1980.

14. Ibid.

15. Munley, *Hospice Alternative*, 275.

16. Barbara Mishkin et al., *Decisions in Hospice*, (Arlington, Va.: The National Hospice Organization, 1985), 12.

17. Ibid.

18. Ibid., 2.

19. Ibid., 8.

20. For further information about hospice care, contact the National Hospice Organization, 1901 North Fort Myer Drive, Suite 402, Arlington, VA 22209, (703) 243-5900.

21. David O. Moberg, "Is Your Church an Honest Ally or a Friendly Foe of the Aged?" *Journal of Christian Education*, September 1982, 51.

22. Tim Stafford, "The Graying of the Church," *Christianity Today*, 6 November 1987, 17.

23. Jean E. Thompson, "Life Care Ministry: The Church as Part of the Elderly Support Network" in *The Role of the Church in Aging* (New York: The Haworth Press, 1986), 65.

24. Ibid., 74.

Conclusion

Forming a Response:
An Action Plan for Individuals, Families, and Churches

*T*his book opened with a series of short case studies showing the difficult medical care decisions one may face at life's end. These examples were not intended to form the basis for any particular response to the dilemmas of treatment and care, but rather to illustrate the intense anguish of such situations. At a time of coping with a crisis of these proportions, it is virtually asking too much to expect the people involved to weigh the philosophical and societal import of particular choices.

There is, however, an ideal time to do just that: anytime before a crisis strikes. Now may be the appropriate time to respond to the critical concerns presented here. In this concluding section, a brief review of the book is followed by suggestions for understanding the debate over treatment and care choices and discerning the right choice for you or your parent or any other loved one who may face a life-threatening illness or condition.

In Part 1, we examined the rapidly changing world of medical technology. Advances in knowledge and ability to fight disease have greatly enhanced our lives, but they have produced a fundamental change in outlook. The physician is now a tech-nocrat—an aggressor against disease. His role is not limited to that of a sympathetic counselor and interpreter of disease. In addition, steep cost escalations are accompanying advances in health care. A subtle attitude shift is becoming apparent as a result: Health-care "consumers" expect a good return on their "investment" in medical know-how; a physician's failure to diagnose or arrest an illness may provoke a malpractice suit. The reality of undeserved pain and suffering, we are led to believe, is intolerable in our day and age.

Western society is placing a premium on physical life and health with little, if any, reference to spiritual well-being or the biblical concept of the sanctity of all life. This mindset places us on a trajectory toward more and more willing accep-tance of a "right to die." It is not so different from abortion, some people rationalize, and that has been legal since 1973. Besides, the elderly have a "duty to die and get out of the way," others say. And once you have lost your health it is senseless to hang onto life any longer. These messages form a persuasive drumbeat of support for assisted suicide and active euthanasia.

Their repercussions are being felt far and wide throughout the American legal system, where difficult cases concerning the termination of medical treatment—and even an end to pro-viding food and water—are debated. To cope with these uncer-tainties, a majority of states have enacted natural death acts, recognizing "living wills" as appropriate means for patients to express ahead of time their desire for care to be terminated under certain circumstances. Nearly everywhere, individuals can designate another person to make treatment decisions on their behalf. Where no such advance arrangements are made, a growing number of states simply allow a guardian or family member to impose treatment decisions on a terminally ill, incompetent patient.

While popular media and the American legal system wrestle with these questions, ethicists and theologians are de-bating them on a deeper, philosophical level. In Part 2, the views of influential participants in the debate were explored. Among them are Joseph Fletcher, advocating a right to die; Roman Catholic moralists insisting on God's timing and the value of suffering; and evangelical C. Everett Koop, standing consistently for the sanctity of life. Koop critiques the euphemism "quality of life," pointing out that utilitarian attitudes toward the terminally ill, handicapped, or elderly reflect a diminished quality of life for the person sitting in judgment.

Biblical precedents for respecting the sanctity of life and church tradition supporting it form the basis for contemporary Christian understandings of death, dying, and suffering. In this context, Part 3 detailed possible responses to the new health-care realities of our day. Planning ahead is crucial at a time when life-sustaining treatments are regularly discontinued for incompetent patients. In many cases, the person making this irrevocable choice is a family member or court-appointed surrogate who may or may not reflect the personal values and desires of the patient.

To avoid this predicament, two vehicles have come into use: the durable power of attorney, appointing a substitute decision maker chosen by the patient; and the living will or advance treatment directive, indicating what sort of treatments should be continued or discontinued in the event of a life-threatening illness or condition. Discussions with clergy, family members, or trusted professionals in the fields of law and medicine may provide a foundation for personal decision making on these issues.

Finally, Part 3 acquainted the reader with an alternative to aggressive hospital treatment at life's end. The option of hospice care provides comfort, companionship, relief from pain, and bereavement counseling for terminal patients and their families. Many communities in the United States have hospice programs available, and often church ministries to elderly people living alone utilize some hospice techniques. Visiting a hospice inpatient unit or volunteering to assist in meeting the needs of dying patients and their families are good ways of learning more about hospice.

There are parallel concerns addressed in this book. First, a compelling need exists for individuals and families to come to grips in advance with treatment choices. Second, as a society we need to cope responsibly with forces pushing us to the brink of accepting not only a right to die, but a right to put to death those deemed to have a diminished "quality of life." Informed individuals taking initiative on behalf of themselves and their loved ones can begin to make a difference. That difference may be multiplied many times as churches educate members, promote discussions of these issues, and model a positive, compassionate, respectful attitude toward elderly and infirm individuals.

Church members and clergy may even want to serve as designated decision-makers for elderly members or others who do not have family members nearby or whose families do not share their convictions. For Christians considering these difficult issues, it is important to understand one reality of contemporary America: Courts throughout the land are deciding that most people would want medical treatment terminated in certain circumstances. Citizens who want to exempt themselves and their loved ones from this emerging legal consensus need to affirm their views in advance. Explaining the source of those views grounded in a Christian world and life view can reflect scriptural truth and values to a society in sore need of hearing more about them.

Personal action and commitment are essential when individual views depart from the worldly norm on these issues. Compare treatment decisions with abortion, for example. Moral opposition to abortion may require no more of an individual than a private decision never to have an abortion. For the present, at least, no one in America needs to fear a coerced abortion. However, the individual may have little or no control over final treatment decisions made for him or her at the end of life. If an incapacitated patient's wishes are not expressed in advance, if trust and specific instructions are not placed with a like-minded relative or friend, there are no guarantees of how—or whether—medical treatment will continue.

Euthanasia is not a solution to the health-care challenges of contemporary society. It emerges out of an orientation to life that downplays God's sovereignty, diminishes the importance of sustaining relationships, and cuts short the search for creative, life-affirming answers for people in distress. It does not have to become entrenched in medical practice, as abortion has, because so many members of the medical profession remain opposed to it. If Christians join in offering alternatives compatible with biblical truth, then the momentum toward deliberate killing may be curbed. The place to begin is at home and at church, with thoughtful, informed discussions of these matters. The time to begin is now.

Appendix 1

CRISTA Nursing Center:
Guidelines Regarding
Life-Sustaining Treatment

*T*hese guidelines apply to the withholding or withdrawing of life support, including cardiopulmonary resuscitation. They were developed with the assistance of a special CRISTA Committee and were approved by the CRISTA Board of Trustees on 25 June 1987.

CHRISTIAN PRINCIPLES

CRISTA, as a Christian institution, affirms the special worth of men and women as reflected in both God's Acts of Creation and Redemption. God created human beings in His "image" with moral, social and spiritual superiority over all other forms of creation. God has redeemed human beings for the purpose of abundant, productive life and with the confident assurance of life "eternal." Because of these convictions, CRISTA will treat each patient with the utmost dignity as one whom God made and loves. We recognize that human beings have the responsibility and privilege to work together with God to exercise judgment concerning maintenance of health; seek to eradicate disease; and to nurture life as a gift from God.

201

CRISTA accepts the Holy Bible as God's word and recognizes this as our authority for faith and practice. CRISTA policy is formulated only after a careful study of biblical teachings. As a result of our consideration of biblical teaching, we affirm that life is ordained and sustained by God. We also recognize that when all reasonable efforts to maintain life are exhausted we recognize that death is the end of the natural process of life. As Christians we also affirm life eternal.

GENERAL GUIDELINES

We affirm the principle that the informed and competent person has the right to refuse or forego treatment. We further recognize that the informed and competent patient is the primary decision-maker for his/her own care.

This does not mean, however, that the patient has unlimited rights. Nothing in CRISTA's policies shall be construed to condone or approve mercy killing (euthanasia), to permit any other action which would be contrary to the laws of the State of Washington.

In general, if it is agreed that the patient's condition is reversible, the presumption is in favor of further treatment. If the prognosis is unclear, the presumption is also in favor of further treatment. If it is irreversible and death is imminent, the withholding or withdrawing of life-sustaining treatment may be a reasonable and prudent consideration.

It is the responsibility of health care professionals to act in the best interest of the patient.

The comfort and dignity of the patient will always be a primary objective.

SPECIFIC GUIDELINES

1. Food, water, and oxygen, as the necessary and natural supports for life, will be provided as long as such provision is not detrimental to other aspects of the patient's physical well-being.

2. Medication, which will relieve pain, will be provided, whenever such provision is not detrimental to other aspects of the patient's physical well-being.

3. Life-sustaining treatments may be introduced, withheld or removed under the specific directives of a competent patient. These decisions and preferences shall be documented in the patient's medical record. In the case of the patient that decides to refuse or forego a specific treatment the following shall be required:

a. The primary physician and two other consulting physicians shall unanimously concur that the illness is irreversible and in the reasonable and prudent opinion of the physicians involved, that death is imminent, and;

b. The primary physician will consult with the primary care nurse for his or her advice and opinion.

4. In the case of the incompetent patient who has not executed an advance directive, the decision to refuse or forego a specific treatment shall require the following:

a. Unanimous written concurrence of the immediate family; or in the event the patient has no immediate family, the concurrence of the duly appointed guardian of the patient.

b. The primary physician along with two other consulting physicians shall unanimously concur that the illness is irreversible and in the reasonable and prudent opinion of the physicians involved, that death is imminent; and

c. The primary physician will consult with the primary care nurse for his or her advice and opinion.

If disagreement persists among those involved in the decision-making process, a patient care conference will be convened with members of the health care team and family, where possible.

If this effort is unsuccessful, the CRISTA Ethics Committee will be consulted for advice and recommendations.

If no resolution can be reached, full care will be continued.

5. If CRISTA is placed in the position of choosing not to comply with a patient directive because of these guidelines, CRISTA shall as promptly as practicable transfer care to another health care facility.

DOCUMENTATION

Upon Admission:

The provision of a properly executed living-will and/or durable power of attorney is encouraged with a copy to become a part of the medical record.

Upon admission, specific directives from the patient or the patient's surrogate shall be recorded in the medical record. These instructions shall include such matters as code status and life-support treatments.

Periodic Reviews:

Patient care conferences shall periodically review and document the specific instructions of the patient.

Maryland Life-Sustaining Procedures Act

Section 5-601. Definitions.

(a) *In general.*—In this subtitle the following words have the meanings indicated.

(b) *Attending physician.*—"Attending physician" means a physician who has been selected by or assigned to, and has primary responsibility for the treatment and care of, a declarant.

(c) *Declarant.*—"Declarant" means an individual who has executed a declaration.

(d) *Declaration.*—"Declaration" means a document that is executed under Section 5-602 or 5-611 of this subtitle.

(e) *Life-sustaining procedure.*—"Life-sustaining procedure" means any medical procedure, treatment, or intervention which uses mechanical or other artificial means to sustain, restore, or supplant a spontaneous vital function or is otherwise of such a nature as to afford a patient no reasonable expectation of recovery from a terminal condition and which when applied to a patient in a terminal condition, would serve to secure only a precarious and burdensome prolongation of life.

(f) *Qualified patient.*—"Qualified patient" means a declarant diagnosed, within a reasonable degree of medical certainty, to be in a terminal condition as certified in writing by 2 physicians, both of whom have personally examined the declarant, and at least 1 of whom is an attending physician of the declarant.

(g) *Terminal condition.*—"Terminal condition" means an incurable condition of a patient caused by injury, disease, or illness which, to a reasonable degree of medical certainty, makes death imminent and from which, despite the application of life-sustaining procedures, there can be no recovery.

Section 5-602. Declaration—In general.

(a) *Requirements.*—Any individual qualified to make a will under Section 4-101 of the Estates and Trusts Article may execute a declaration, as provided in subsection (c) of this section, directing the withholding or withdrawal of life-sustaining procedures under this subtitle. The declaration shall be:

(1) Voluntary;

(2) Dated and in writing;

(3) Signed by the declarant or, if at the declarant's expressed direction and in the declarant's presence, by another individual on behalf of the declarant;

(4) Executed in the presence of and attested by at least 2 witnesses each of whom, at the time or execution, is at least 18 years old and is not:

(i) An individual who signed the declaration at the direction and on behalf of the declarant under paragraph (3) of this subsection;

(ii) Related to the declarant by blood or marriage within a degree listed under Section 2-202 of the Family Law Article;

(iii) Either a creditor of the declarant or knowingly entitled to any portion of the estate of the declarant under any existing testamentary instrument of the declarant or knowingly entitled to any financial benefit by reason of the death of the declarant; or

(iv) Financially or otherwise responsible for

the declarant's medical care or an employee of any such person or institution.

(b) *Notice to physician.*—(1) A declarant is responsible for notifying the attending physician of the existence of the declaration either directly or through another individual.

(2) Notice may be given by delivery of the declaration or a copy of the declaration to the attending physician.

(3) The attending physician shall make the declaration or other written documents containing a declaration in conformance with the provisions of paragraph (c) (1) of this section a part of the declarant's medical records.

(c) *Form.*—(1) The declaration shall be substantially in the following form:

"DECLARATION

On this _____ day of _____ (month, year), I, _____ being of sound mind, willfully and voluntarily direct that my dying shall not be artificially prolonged under the circumstances set forth in this declaration:

If at any time I should have an incurable injury, disease, or illness certified to be a terminal condition by two (2) physicians who have personally examined me, one (1) of whom shall be my attending physician, and the physicians have determined that my death is imminent and will occur whether or not life-sustaining procedures are utilized and where the application of such procedures would serve only to artificially prolong the dying process, I direct that such procedures be withheld or withdrawn, and that I be permitted to die naturally with only the administration of medication, the administration of food and water, and the performance of any medical procedure that is necessary to provide comfort care or alleviate pain. In the absence of my ability to give directions regarding the use of such life-sustaining procedures, it is my intention that this declaration shall be honored by my family and physician(s) as the final expression of my right to control my medical care and treatment.

I am legally competent to make this declaration, and I understand its full import.

Signed _____

Address _____

_____

Under penalty of perjury, we state that this declaration was signed by _____ in the presence of the under-signed who, at _____ request, in _____ _____ presence, and in the presence of each other, have hereunto signed our names as witnesses this _____ day of _____, 19_____. Further, each of us, individually, states that: The declarant is known to me, and I believe the declarant to be of sound mind. I did not sign the declarant's signature to this declaration. Based upon information and belief, I am not related to the declarant by blood or marriage, a creditor of the declarant, entitled to any portion of the estate of the declarant under any existing testamentary instrument of the declarant, entitled to any financial benefit by reason of the death of the declarant, financially or otherwise responsible for the declarant's medical care, nor an employee of any such person or institution.

_____ Address _____

_____

_____ Address _____

_____

(2) The declaration may include additional provisions on this or other subjects that are not inconsistent with other provisions of this subtitle. If any additional provisions are declared invalid, the invalidity does not affect the validity of the declaration or of other provisions which can be given effect without the invalid provision, and to this end the provisions in the declaration are severable.

Section 5-603. Same—Revocation.

A declarant may revoke a declaration at any time by:

(1) A written statement to that effect:

(i) Signed and dated by the declarant; or

(ii) If the statement so indicates, signed and dated by a person acting at the direction of the declarant.

(2) An expression to that effect, after the declarant knows of the disease, illness, or injury involved in any question regarding the existence of a terminal condition;

(3) Destroying the declaration;

(4) Marking, burning, tearing, or otherwise altering, defacing, or damaging the declaration in a manner indicating the intention to revoke it.

Section 5-604. Required actions by attending physician.

(a) *Attending physicians of declarants in terminal condition.*—Subject to the provisions of subsection (b) and (c) of this section and if the declarant is unable to give directions regarding the use of life-sustaining procedures, the attending physician or a declarant in a terminal condition shall promptly:

(1) Take the actions necessary to provide for the certification required for the declarant to become a qualified patient; and

(2) Upon certification, implement the declaration.

(b) *Transfer of the declarant to other physician.*—An attending physician who does not comply with subsection (a) of this section shall make every reasonable effort to transfer the declarant to another physician.

(c) *Revoked declarations.*—Subsection (a) of this section does not apply if the attending physician knows that the declaration has been revoked or for so long as the physician has a reasonable basis for believing that the declaration may have been revoked.

(d) *Basis for physician's conclusion placed in medical records.*—The attending physician shall place in the declarant's medical records the evidentiary basis for the physician's conclusion:

(1) That a valid and unrevoked declaration exists if the physician acts under subsection (a) of this section; or

(2) That the declaration has been revoked or may have been revoked if the physician acts under subsection (c) of this section.

Section 5-605. When declaration may not be implemented.

The declaration of a qualified patient to withhold or withdraw life-sustaining procedures may not be implemented:

(1) By the denial of food, water, or of such medication and medical procedures as are necessary to provide comfort care and to alleviate pain; or

(2) If the qualified patient is pregnant.

Section 5-606. Declaration presumed valid.

In the absence of evidence to the contrary, a declaration which, on its face, satisfies the requirements of Section 5-602 or 5-611 of this subtitle is presumed to be valid.

Section 5-607. Withholding or withdrawing of life-sustaining procedures.

(a) *Civil liability*.—Except as provided in subsection (b) or subsection (c) of this section, on notification of the existence of a valid declaration any person who causes a failure to comply with the provisions of Section 5-604 may be held civilly liable.

(b) *Certain health care providers not liable*.—A paid or volunteer fire fighter, paramedic, or member of an ambulance or rescue squad is not subject to criminal or civil liability for aid, care, or assistance rendered in good faith and under reasonable standards to a qualified patient, even if that aid, care, or assistance is contrary to the provisions of that qualified patient's declaration.

(c) *Liability of nonprofessionals*.—(1) A person who in good faith, pursuant to reasonable medical standards, and in accordance with the requirements of this subtitle, causes or participates in the withholding or withdrawing of life-sustaining procedures from a qualified patient:

(i) Is not subject to civil or criminal liability; and

(ii) May not be found to have committed professional misconduct.

(2) The provisions of paragraph (1) of this subsection do not:

(i) Apply to any acts or omissions prior to the time a declarant becomes a qualified patient; or

(ii) Exempt any person from liability or professional responsibility for willful or wanton misconduct or for negligence.

Section 5-608. Conditional execution of declaration.

A person or other legal entity may not require execution of a declaration as a condition for providing shelter, insurance coverage, or health care benefits or services.

Section 5-609. Prohibited actions by life insurers.

A life insurer, as defined in Article 48A of the Code, because of the execution or implementation of a declaration under this subtitle, may not:

(1) Decline to provide or continue coverage to the declarant;

(2) Consider the terms of an existing policy of life insurance to have been breached or modified; or

(3) Invoke any suicide or intentional death exemption or exclusion in any policy covering the declarant.

Section 5-610. Provisions cumulative; presumption of intent for individuals not executing declaration; construction of provisions.

The provisions of the subtitle:

(1) Are cumulative and may not be construed to impair or supersede any legal right or responsibility that any

person may have to effect the initiation, continuation, withholding, or withdrawal of life-sustaining procedures;

(2) Do not create a presumption concerning the intention of an individual who is in a terminal condition and who has not executed a declaration regarding the initiation, continuation, withholding, or withdrawal of life-sustaining procedures; and

(3) May not be construed to permit any affirmative or deliberate act or omission to end life other than to permit the withholding or withdrawing of life-sustaining procedures from a declarant in a terminal condition.

Section 5-611. Declaration for initiation or continuation of life-sustaining procedures.

An individual who is qualified to make a will under Section 4-101 of the Estates and Trusts Article, in lieu of a declaration directing the withholding or withdrawal of life-sustaining procedures, may execute a declaration directing the initiation or continuation of life-sustaining procedures in accordance with standard medical practice.

Section 5-612. Execution of more than one declaration; declarations executed outside State.

(a) *Only last executed declaration given effect.*—If an individual validly executes more than 1 declaration under this subtitle, only the last executed declaration shall be given effect.

(b) *Declarations executed outside State by nonresidents.*—A declaration that is executed outside of this State by a nonresident shall be given effect in this state if that declaration is in compliance with the provisions of this subtitle.

Section 5-613. Acts authorized by subtitle not considered suicide, violation of criminal law, or standard of professional conduct.

An act authorized by this subtitle may not, for any purpose, be considered to be a suicide or a violation of any criminal law or standard of professional conduct.

Section 5-614. Forgeries and other prohibited acts.

Any person who forges a revocation or a declaration, or who willfully purports by any of the other methods set forth in Section 5-603 of this subtitle to revoke a declaration without the consent of the declarant, or who wilfully conceals or withholds personal knowledge of a revocation is guilty of a misdemeanor and on conviction is subject to a fine not exceeding $1,000.

Subject Index